10649611

GOLDEN OLDIES

STEVE PROPES

"GOLDEN "OLDIES"

A Guide to 60's
Record Collecting

CHILTON BOOK COMPANY
Radnor, Pennsylvania

FA

R 016.7899

Propes

Copyright © 1974 by Stephen C. Propes

First Edition   *All Rights Reserved*

Published in Radnor, Pa., by Chilton Book Company
and simultaneously in Ontario, Canada
by Thomas Nelson & Sons, Ltd.

Designed by Anne Churchman

Manufactured in the United States of America

Fine Arts

Library of Congress Cataloging in Publication Data

Propes, Steve.
  Golden oldies; a guide to 60's record collecting.

  "The recordings discussed are . . . rhythm and blues and rock and
roll 45 RPM singles."
  1. Music, Popular (Songs, etc.)—United States—Discography. 2.
Phonorecord collecting. I. Title.
ML156.4.P6P75   016.7899'12   74-4102
ISBN 0-8019-6062-2
ISBN 0-8019-6076-2 (pbk.)

ACKNOWLEDGMENTS

Thanks to Greg Shaw of *Phonograph Record* magazine
and to Joanie Grant of Motown for their help.

To
CLARENCE AND AILEEN
with love

PREFACE

Popular music of the 1960's, like the decade itself, was a constantly changing form. Those recordings and recording artists that best characterize the changing sounds of this volatile era, during which rhythm and blues evolved into soul music and rock and roll into rock music, are the main concern of this book. *Golden Oldies* is directed to the beginning 60's record collector and written from the viewpoint of the 60's single record collector. The recordings discussed are the rhythm and blues and rock and roll 45 RPM singles that are among the most sought after. They comprise the representative best of 60's popular music.

CONTENTS

x *Contents*

RECORD COLLECTING

•

Collecting 60's music is not as profitable, nor as "nostalgic," as collecting late 40's and 50's rhythm and blues and rock and roll records. Yet 60's music has already attracted a substantial coterie of authorities and dedicated collectors, and the number is sure to grow as that decade becomes "the good old days."

Subgroups of 60's collectors proliferate, restricting themselves to narrow confines of recorded music. Among these subgroups are the collector of British Rock, with the even more specialized Beatles collector. The Beatles collector seeks not only records, but also all 45 RPM record picture sleeves (the sleeve to "Can't Buy Me Love" is the rarest), and other fringe material including obscure recordings of Lennon-McCartney compositions and all records by early ex-Beatle Pete Best. Other specialists are the surf-rock collector, containing the Beach Boys subgroup; the Bob Dylan collector, also seeking out little-known Dylan compositions by other artists; and the Phil Spector collector (the rhyme is inadvertent, the Phil Spector and Philles label fanatic is for real) to name just a few.

The Long Play Versus the 45 RPM Record

The 60's was an era of change in the presentation and packaging of popular music. During the 50's and the early

60's, great emphasis was placed upon the hit potential of the 45 RPM single. However, by 1965 the long play (LP) album had become the primary medium for recording performances of rock music and, to a lesser extent, soul music. The Beatles focused newfound attention on the LP with their "Sergeant Pepper's Lonely Hearts Club Band" LP (Capitol 2653), which is not a simple series of individual LP tracks, but an innovative long play art form—one record with the various tracks developing into a self-contained theme and identity. This concept differed radically from the bulk of previous rock and roll LP's, which had been a generally haphazard compilation of songs on one record.

New attention to the long play rock record increased air play for rock music on newly programmed "underground" FM radio stations heavily specializing in rock LP's and LP tracks.

During this renaissance of the LP, the 45 RPM single persisted and inadvertently became a barometer of changing tastes in rock music. Record companies had originally intended the 45 RPM single to be a throwaway item released merely to hype sales of the all-important LP—not to primarily sustain itself on sales as a hit single record. But because the 45 RPM single was used to enhance the more profitable LP sales, more often than not, it represented the best of the LP, the distilled essence of the entire work, and this resulted in a series of single releases constituting a hard-core best of rock. Ironically, removing the burden of proving and sustaining itself from the single led to an era of excellent single recordings.

Scarcity of 60's Records

Deleting records from their current 45 RPM catalog is an almost universal practice among record companies. This occurs generally only a few months from the original date of issue. The most successful hits are deleted in the original issue form and then reissued as singles on a "greatest hits" or "back-to-back" series. The original label pressing of any given record is therefore only available for an extremely short period of time. Even recent releases, if few enough were pressed, become scarce within a surprisingly short time.

Bootlegs

Bootlegs, a real factor in 50's record collecting, are to date nearly nonexistent as far as 60's 45 RPM singles are concerned. The market for the bootlegged 45 from the 60's is currently quite limited, but if experience is a teacher they will no doubt appear more often as the originals become increasingly rare. Bootlegged recordings are a notorious aspect of the rock LP market, featuring such top flight artists as The Beatles, The Rolling Stones and Bob Dylan.

Bootleggers of 50's recordings are often collectors who faithfully copy the original label design and use colored vinyl in the pressing. Preferring to identify the product as a "reproduction," they sell these records for from $3 to $5 apiece. In contrast, the 60's 45 RPM bootleg is usually pressed on cheap polystyrene from scratchy originals and given an austere label design.

Sources for Original Records

There is fierce competition among collectors of the 45 RPM record for the rhythm and blues and rock and roll discs pressed in the 1950's. Equally fine 45 RPM records released in the 60's are often overlooked. However, increased interest in the 60's era has attracted some healthy competition for scarce soul and rock recordings from the decade.

Though original label 45 RPM issues of most 60's records are no longer pressed, these recordings can be obtained through various sources.

Secondhand / Thrift Stores

The experienced record collector has long been able to locate many of his wants at a low cost through frequent visits to secondhand, rummage and thrift stores, garage sales and swap-meets.

The chief disadvantage of thrift shop collecting is that in many cases the records located have been played a lot. As with 50's record collecting, the buyer should carefully note unusual wear, warpage or hairline cracks. In many cases, if a collector bypasses a good-selling 60's record in inferior condition, chances are good that he'll soon locate the same disc in much better shape. If the worn record is obscure, it is often advisable to purchase the less than perfect copy.

A uniform system of grading 45's is used by most 50's record collectors. It's just as applicable to 60s' 45 RPM records.

Condition		Description
Mint	(M)	An unplayed record with no defects.
Very Good	(VG)	A record with very slight surface noise, resulting from very little play. This record has been stored in a sleeve and has been handled with care.
Good	(G)	This record is in average condition and has been played frequently. There is some surface noise. Many collectors find this grade satisfactory.
Fair	(F)	This record has been used. The distortion equals the recorded performance. The record can be enjoyed only with effort.
Poor	(P)	The distortion exceeds the recorded performance. This record is unsatisfactory for listening purposes.

There are variations to these grades, generally indicated by a plus (+) or minus (−). Thus a record in G+ condition is slightly more worn than a record in VG− condition. Of course, these grades vary according to the judgment and perception of the grader.

Retail / Wholesale Sources

Records in mint condition can often be obtained through sales of discontinued 45's held in discount stores, five and dime locations, record shops and other retail outlets. Record jobbers, distributors and jukebox dealers occasionally sell discontinued stock, but they often insist on minimum purchases.

Collectors Magazines / Auction Lists

Another method of locating original issue 45's is through sales and auctions held by other collectors and record dealers. Though a winning bid in an auction is generally well above the thrift store or retail price, this is an excellent way of obtaining hard to get records. Auctions abound in collectors' magazines and privately mailed lists.

During the first few years of the 70's, there were no less than five major magazines designed for collectors of 50's and 60's rhythm and blues and rock and roll. As of 1974, only two of these journals survive.

Bim Bam Boom. Box 301, Bronx, N.Y. 10469. Articles on rhythm and blues and rock and roll artists of the 50's and 60's. Excellent, extensive auction and sale lists.

Record Exchanger. Box 2144, Anaheim, Calif. 92804. Also concerned with 50's and 60's rock and roll and rhythm and blues. The extensive auction and sale lists are by consignment only.

Two other magazines feature articles on 50's and 60's records, but do not concentrate on record auctions or sales.

Shout. 46 Slades Dr., Chislehurst, Kent BR 7 6JX, England. An excellent source for information on 60's and 70's soul music.

Stormy Weather. Box 2837, Oakland, Calif. 94618. Articles on records and artists of the 50's and 60's. Undergoes constant format changes, making every irregularly printed issue a surprise package.

DOMINANT THEMES IN 60'S MUSIC
•

Several themes popular in the late 50's carried over into the music of the early 60's, from 1960 through 1963.

Dance Records

The Olympics' "Hully Gully" was a 1959 hit, yet it continued to sell consistently until 1960 and beyond. The success of the "Hully Gully" shows the strength of the straightforward, uncluttered dance record, devoid of pretension or social comment.

Without a doubt, the biggest dance record of the early 60's was another 50's-derived product: "The Twist" was drawn from the 1959 recording by Hank Ballard and The Midnighters (King 5171) and transformed into a major 1960 and 1962 hit by Chubby Checker (Parkway 811). Checker was a little-known rock and roll performer whose one previous release, "The Class" (Parkway 804), was a rhythm and blues equivalent to "The Chipmunk Song"—with "Charlie Brown" as the pest. However, with the enormous success of "The Twist," Checker recorded a string of early 60's dance hits.

"The Twist" was far from the only successful record of this period. Enjoying brief surges of popularity were "The Watusi" by The Vibrations, "The Wah-Watusi" by The Orlons, the "Hitch Hike" by Marvin Gaye, "The Dog" by

7

Rufus Thomas and "The Bounce" by The Olympics. Championed mainly by Rufus Thomas, The Olympics and Mitch Ryder and The Detroit Wheels, the classic dance record enjoyed limited popularity throughout the 60's. This form of rock and roll was deceptively innocent and gave no hint of the beginning tumultuous musical changes.

Summer Lifestyle

The summer lifestyle theme was best portrayed by the uniquely 60's "surf-rock" form. The major exponents of this California rock and roll style were The Beach Boys, whose first release, "Surfin'," was a simple celebration of this warm weather sport. With The Beach Boys' next major surf hits, "Surfin' Safari" and "Surfin' U.S.A.," came two excellent fast car flip sides, the exciting "Shut Down" and "409." This fast car theme was partially derived from cruising and fast car recordings by The Medallions and other 50's rhythm and blues vocal groups. Instrumentals such as "Wild Weekend" by The Rockin' Rebels, "Boss" by The Rumblers and "Whittier Blvd." by The Midniters were essentially surf-rock instrumentals that became popular cruising records because cruising is ideally suited to dominant guitar rock and roll music. Rhythm and blues groups adapted the summertime theme to urban experiences with Martha and The Vandellas' "Dancing In The Street" and with "Up On The Roof" and "Under The Boardwalk," both by The Drifters. These records expressively portrayed big city summertime activities. "Groovin'," a 1966 Rascals hit, was a good-time, relaxed-tempo summertime happening.

Nonviolent Rebellion

Representing a not quite serious, yet slightly self-conscious view of teenage life at the birth of 60's rebellion,

"He's A Rebel" by The Crystals, "Leader Of The Pack" by The Shangri-La's and "Stubborn Kind of Fellow" by Marvin Gaye revealed a benignly rebellious spirit. Several years later, this theme would develop into an unequivocal statement of violence. However, this was 1962, the year that Carole King's composition, "He Hit Me (And It Felt Like A Kiss)," by The Crystals was suppressed because of suggested violence. The themes of mid-60's rock and roll reflected a loss of innocence, and yet certain subjects remained off-limits.

Implied Sex / Drugs

In the mid-60's, undisguised recorded statements of controversial subjects were efficiently suppressed. "Stoned" by The Rolling Stones was nothing more than a blues-rock instrumental. Its solitary lyric was the title word at the record's beginning, but apparently the drug implication was strong enough, and the record was very quickly removed from the American market.

The Stones returned with the major 1965 hit, "Satisfaction," with implied sexual overtones; "Day Tripper" by The Beatles had similar implications, but neither record was a direct-on sexual statement. The Beatles' "Yellow Submarine" was an early hit record with vague references to perceptions gained through psychedelics, but the message remained implicit.

Rebellion

An outgrowth of early 60's protest records and the understated violence of such early rhythm and blues groups as The Crystals and The Shangri-La's, the subject of rebellion was more sharply defined in the mid-60's. This theme was expressed in at least two ways: undisguised advocacy of violence or defiance of authority; subtle, clearly satirical lyrics.

"Sic 'Em Pigs" by Canned Heat presented strongly anti-police lyrics and made little attempt to mask this controversial theme. "Street Fighting Man" by The Rolling Stones adapted the sound of Martha and The Vandellas' "Dancing In The Street" and turned it into a tough, jarring recorded street fight—a truly violent rock encounter. Satirists were more devastating than the harsher advocates of violence. Some British groups were particularly effective at satire: The Kinks' releases, "A Well Respected Man" and "Dedicated Follower Of Fashion," and Manfred Mann's "Semi-Detached Suburban Mr. James" found an easily recognized mark. Middle-class complacency, an ideal target for newly emerging rock artists, was also dealt with in The Animals' "We've Got To Get Out Of This Place," The Beatles' "Nowhere Man" and Bob Dylan's "Positively 4th Street." The Who's "My Generation" was rebellious in execution, yet it communicated more of a pro-youth message than an anti-establishment theme.

Unity and Solidarity

Several groups expressed an outspoken theme of unity. The Animals' "Don't Let Me Be Misunderstood" was a self-doubting teenage plea much in the spirit of George Hamilton IV's 1958 hit, "Why Don't They Understand" (ABC 9862). Unity was also the dominant theme of The Van Dykes' "No Man Is An Island" and The Youngbloods' "Get Together"—an anthem for a youthful generation seeking a common ground. "For What It's Worth" by The Buffalo Springfield was a narrative of violence, specifically of the youth-versus-police riots on the Sunset Strip, and as such it became a well-expressed statement that riots and violence aren't inevitable.

Civil Rights

Themes with serious social impact were effectively rendered by The Impressions in "I've Been Trying," "People

Get Ready" and in the religiously derived "Amen," all exceptional compositions by lead singer Curtis Mayfield. Joe Tex, who frequently recorded novelty lyrics, issued the hopeful and progressive "I Believe I'm Gonna Make It."

Explicit Sex/Drugs

During the late 60's, lyrics and messages were rendered in a more outspoken and unmistakable fashion.

The subject of sex, only hinted at during the mid-60's, was boldly expressed in "Let's Spend The Night Together" by The Rolling Stones. However, in the tradition of 50's prudish timidity, top-40 radio banned the record, and the bland, ballad flip, "Ruby Tuesday" became a major Stones' hit.

Soon thereafter, several brilliant singles were released—records so undeniably good that suppression was impossible. The Doors' "Light My Fire" was a potent sexual message with an equally strong drug message. This double message was also evident in Sly and The Family Stone's "I Want To Take You Higher." These powerful single recordings paved the way for the acceptance of such later releases as the psychedelic trips, "Itchycoo Park" by The Small Faces, "Cloud Nine" by The Temptations and "Magic Carpet Ride" by Steppenwolf and the somber yet hallucinogenic expressions of Procol Harum's "A Whiter Shade of Pale," The Doors' "People Are Strange" and The Jefferson Airplane's "White Rabbit."

Introspective Protest

The war in Viet Nam, universally condemned by youth, was proclaimed at an end in The Doors' "The Unknown Soldier." The Plastic Ono Band's "Give Peace A Chance" made much the same statement and stressed a loving appeal for a peaceful humanity.

Social Consciousness

One likable strength of 50's rhythm and blues and rock and roll was the perfect match of easy, unpretentious lyrics with generally direct-on vocal deliveries. With exceptions, 50's pop music dealt with problems on a strictly personal level, attempting neither a point of view nor an expression of opinion. By the later 60's, rock music and soul music began taking stances and expanding to social problems, often at the expense of the simple power inherent in the music.

This theme of social consciousness took several distinct forms: a lyric which provided a lesson or advice; a lyric of affirmation or pride; and a lyric dealing with interracial relationships.

The lesson provided by James Brown in 1966 was "Don't Be A Drop-Out," obvious yet sound advice. Having arrived as a major soul superstar, Brown sought to correct inequity through his rather blunt "message" recordings and put himself in the forefront of this didactic approach to social change. Elvis Presley's "In The Ghetto" and Diana Ross and The Supremes' "Love Child" also expressed timely social themes with direct object lessons.

The theme of affirmation was perhaps most effective within the mode of social consciousness. Especially fine were several releases by The Impressions. "We're A Winner" and "We're Rolling On" were both joyous, rollicking Chi-town vocals. Though somewhat preachy, "This Is My Country" by The Impressions was a sincerely felt statement. "Friendship Train" by Gladys Knight and The Pips and "People Got To Be Free" by The Rascals were slickly upbeat productions with affirmative social messages. Again, James Brown produced the definitive lyric of affirmation in "Say It Loud—I'm Black & I'm Proud," the soul music classic of pride and affirmation. Pride and a strong expression of virility—a dominant 50's theme—were boldly expressed in James Brown's "It's A Man's Man's Man's World," "Respect" by Otis Redding (and later by Aretha Franklin), "Only The Strong Survive" by Jerry

Butler, "Soul Man" by Sam and Dave, "Who's Making Love" by Johnnie Taylor and in such rock releases as "U.S. Male" by Elvis Presley, "Born To Be Wild" by Steppenwolf and "Jumpin' Jack Flash" by The Rolling Stones.

The theme of interracial relationships was delicately expressed in Bobby Taylor and The Vancouvers' sweetly sung "Does Your Mama Know About Me." This theme is also found in Sly and The Family Stone's "Everyday People" and in The Impressions' "Choice Of Colors," with the flip side provocatively entitled "Mighty Mighty (Spade And Whitey)."

Rock Lifestyle

Entirely unique to the superstar conscious era of the late 60's, the theme of the rock lifestyle represented a self-portrait of the rock performer. The Byrds' "So You Want To Be A Rock And Roll Star" is an early, tongue-in-cheek statement, while their later "Bad Night At The Whiskey" is a more serious approach to the same theme. Creedence Clearwater Revival's "Lodi" is an introspective remembrance of the group's early days, and "Travelin' Band" deals with the hassles of touring and one-night stands. Sly and The Family Stone's "Everybody Is A Star" applied the superstar label to the universe of youth. One of the last singles recorded by The Beatles was the excellent, controversial rock and roll release, "The Ballad Of John And Yoko," which explored the disruptions and distractions experienced by the soon-to-be-dissolved Beatles.

Rhythm and Blues Soul Music

Rhythm and blues carried over from the 50's to become the soul music of the post-1965 era. Discussed in the following sections are the styles and single recordings of important rhythm and blues and soul music single artists and vocal groups of the 60's. In several instances where these recordings have already attracted value, there will be short sections on scarcity and relative value.

EARLY 60'S RHYTHM AND BLUES ARTISTS
•

Two very influential rhythm and blues vocalists of the 50's took on a more "pop," middle-of-the-road approach during the early 60's. Jackie Wilson recorded up-tempo rhythm and blues singles along with vocals with a big band sound. Ray Charles recorded jazz and very successful country and western singles. Conversely, Sam Cooke, who specialized in lightweight pop singles in the late 50's, turned towards solid rhythm and blues in the 60's.

Ray Charles

Ray Charles is a truly powerful artist who is fully capable of recording effectively in a very broad range of vocal and instrumental styles. Early in his career, Charles recorded some fine city blues. He progressed into great rock and roll during the late 50's, and after signing with ABC/Paramount Records in 1960, he began experimenting with new recording styles.

His two singles for the Impulse label (an ABC subsidiary) were strictly jazz arrangements. An initial ABC label issue was the bluesy, solidly upbeat "Sticks And Stones." "Hit The Road Jack" in 1961 and "Hide Nor Hair" in 1962 were also in style. Ray Charles' third issue on ABC was the extremely popular country music rendition of the ballad, "Georgia On My Mind." This adaptation of country and western material, complete with a saccharine-sweet background, proved enormously successful in the 1962 hit, "I Can't Stop Loving You." Ray Charles then moved into a big band phase with "Busted" in 1963 and the country-flavored "Crying Time" in 1965. By 1966 Ray Charles had returned to basic rhythm and blues with the effective blues-styled "Let's Go Get Stoned" and the fast-tempo "I Don't Need No Doctor." In 1968, Charles recorded the deadpan, satirical "Understanding," a best-seller. Ray Charles' changing approaches to material and styles reflected the evolution of 60's rhythm and blues—from jazz and popular single releases in the early 60's, to blues-based rock and roll in the later 60's.

Single Releases

Atlantic

976	"Roll With My Baby"/"The Midnight Hour"	1952
984	"Jumpin' In The Mornin' "/"Sun's Gonna Shine Again"	1953
999	"Mess Around"/"Funny"	
1008	"Feelin' Sad"/"Heartbreaker"	
1021	"It Should've Been Me"/"Sinner's Prayer"	1954
1037	"Don't You Know"/"Losing Hand"	
1050	"I've Got A Woman"/"Come Back"	
1063	"This Little Girl Of Mine"/"A Fool For You"	1955
1076	"Greenbacks"/"Blackjack"	
1085	"Drown In My Own Tears"/"Mary Ann"	1956
1096	"Hallelujah I Love Her So"/"What Would I Do Without You"	
1108	"Leave My Woman Alone"/"Lonely Avenue"	
1124	"Ain't That Love"/"I Want To Know"	1957
1143	"It's All Right"/"Get On The Right Track Baby"	
1154	"Swanee River Rock"/"I Want A Little Girl"	
1172	"Talking About You"/"What Kind Of Man Are You"	1958
1180	"Yes Indeed"/"I Had A Dream"	

1196	"You Be My Baby"/"My Bonnie"	
2006	"Rockhouse Pt. 1 & 2"	1959
2010	"The Right Time"/"Tell All The World About You"	
2022	"That's Enough"/"Tell Me How Do You Feel"	
2031	"What'd I Say Pt. 1 & 2"	
2043	"I'm Movin' On"/"I Believe To My Soul"	
2047	"Let The Good Times Roll"/"Don't Let The Sun Catch You Cryin' "	1960
2055	"Just For A Thrill"/"Heartbreaker"	
2068	"Tell The Truth"/"Sweet Sixteen Bars"	
2084	"Come Rain Or Come Shine"/"Tell Me You'll Wait For Me" (also on Atlantic 2470)	
2094	"Early In The Mornin' "/"A Bit Of Soul"	1961
2106	"It Should've Been Me"/"Am I Blue"	
2118	"Hard Times"/"I Wonder Who"	
2174	"Feelin' Sad"/"Carrying That Load"	1963
2239	"Talkin' About You"/"In A Little Spanish Town"	

Impulse

200	"One Mint Julep"/"Let's Go"	1961
202	"I'm Gonna Move To The Outskirts Of Town"/"I've Got News For You"	

ABC

10081	"My Baby"/"Who You Gonna Love"	1960
10118	"Sticks And Stones"/"Worried Life Blues"	
10135	"Georgia On My Mind"/"Carry Me Back To Old Virginny"	
10141	"Them That Got"/"I Wonder"	1961
10164	"Hardhearted Hannah"/"Ruby"	
10244	"Hit The Road Jack"/"The Danger Zone"	
10266	"Unchain My Heart"/"But On The Other Hand Baby"	
10298	"We'll Be Together Again"/"Baby It's Cold Outside" (with Betty Carter)	1962
10314	"Hide Nor Hair"/"At The Club"	
10330	"I Can't Stop Loving You"/"Born To Lose"	
10345	"You Don't Know Me"/"Careless Love"	

10375	"You Are My Sunshine"/"Your Cheating Heart"	
10405	"Don't Set Me Free"/"The Brightest Smile In Town"	1963
10435	"Take These Chains From My Heart"/"No Letter Today"	
10453	"No One"/"Without Love"	
10481	"Busted"/"Make Believe"	
10509	"That Lucky Old Sun"/"Ol' Man Time"	
10530	"Baby Don't You Cry"/"My Heart Cries For You"	1964
10557	"Something's Wrong"/"My Baby Don't Dig Me"	
10571	"No One To Cry To"/"A Tear Fell"	
10588	"Smack Dab In The Middle"/"I Wake Up Crying"	
10609	"Makin' Whoopee Pt. 1 & 2"	
10615	"Cry"/"Teardrops From My Eyes"	1965
10649	"I Gotta Woman Pt. 1 & 2"	
10700	"I'm A Fool To Care"/"Love's Gonna Live Here"	
10720	"The Cincinnati Kid"/"That's All I Am To You"	
10739	"Crying Time"/"When My Dream Boat Comes Home"	
10785	"Together Again"/"You're Just About To Lose Your Clown"	1966
10808	"Let's Go Get Stoned"/"The Train"	
10840	"I Chose To Sing The Blues"/"Hopelessly"	
10865	"I Don't Need No Doctor"/"Please Say You're Fooling"	
10901	"Something Inside Me"/"I Want To Talk About You"	1967
10938	"Somebody Ought To Write A Book About It"/"Here We Go Again"	
10970	"In The Heat Of The Night"/"Something's Got To Change"	
11009	"Yesterday"/"Never Had Enough Of Nothing Yet"	

Jackie Wilson

The versatility and glossy voice of Jackie Wilson proved perfect for styles ranging from basic rhythm and blues to highly commercial soul and popular music. Jackie Wilson began his long recording career with The Dominoes of the early 50's. His first release as a single artist was the rhythmic, expressively sung "Reet Petite." Wilson's ability to spark excitement in his work is apparent in his up-tempo hits of the late 50's, "Lonely Teardrops" in 1958 and "That's Why" in 1959, and in his 60's smash hits, "Baby Workout" in 1963, "Whispers" in 1966 and "Higher And Higher" in 1967. His ability with the melancholy ballad is just as exceptional, as witness the remarkable blues grabber, "Doggin' Around." In the mid-60's, Wilson's style was becoming increasingly subdued, and he recorded such standard material as "Danny Boy" and "I Believe," complete with middle-of-the-road arrangements.

Single Releases

Brunswick
55024   "Reet Petite"/"By The Light Of The Silvery   1957
            Moon"

55052	"To Be Loved"/"Come Back To Me"	1958
55070	"As Long As I Live"/"I'm Wanderin'"	
55086	"Singing A Song"/"We Have Love"	
55105	"Lonely Teardrops"/"In The Blue Of The Evening"	
55121	"That's Why"/"Love Is All"	1959
55136	"I'll Be Satisfied"/"Ask"	
55149	"You Better Know It"/"Never Go Away"	
55165	"Talk That Talk"/"Only You And Only Me"	
55166	"Doggin' Around"/"Night"	1960
55167	"A Woman, A Lover, A Friend"/"All My Love"	
55170	"Am I The Man"/"Alone At Last"	
55201	"My Empty Arms"/"Tear Of The Year"	
55208	"Please Tell Me Why"/"Your One And Only Love"	1961
55216	"I'm Comin' On Back To You"/"Lonely Life"	
55219	"Years From Now"/"You Don't Know What It Means"	
55220	"The Way I Am"/"My Heart Belongs To Only You"	
55221	"There'll Be No Next Time"/"The Greatest Hurt"	1962
55224	"I Found Love" (with Linda Hopkins)	
55225	"Sing"/"Hearts"	
55229	"I Just Can't Help It"/"My Tale Of Woe"	
55233	"Baby That's All"/"Forever And A Day"	
55239	"Baby Workout"/"I'm Going Crazy"	1963
55243	"Shake A Hand"/"Say I Do" (with Linda Hopkins)	
55246	"Shake Shake Shake"/"He's A Fool"	
55250	"Baby Get It"/"The New Breed"	
55254	"Silent Night"/"O Holy Night"	
55260	"Haunted House"/"I'm Travelin' On"	1964
55266	"Big Boss Line"/"Be My Girl"	
55269	"Squeeze Her—Tease Her"/"Give Me Back My Heart"	
55277	"Danny Boy"/"Soul Time"	1965
55280	"No Pity"/"I'm So Lonely"	

55283	"I Believe I'll Love On"/"Lonely Teardrops"	
55287	"Think Twice"/"Please Don't Hurt Me" (with LaVern Baker)	
55289	"3 Days, 1 Hour, 30 Minutes"/"I've Got To Get Back"	
55290	"Brand New Things"/"Soul Galore"	1966
55294	"I Believe"/"Be My Love"	
55300	"Whispers"/"The Fairest Of Them All"	
55309	"I Don't Want To Lose You"/"Just Be Sincere"	1967
55321	"I've Lost You"/"Those Heartaches"	
55336	"Higher And Higher"/"I'm The One To Do It"	
55354	"Since You Showed Me How To Be Happy"/ "The Who Who Song"	
55365	"For Your Precious Love"/"Uptight"	1968
55373	"Chain Gang"/"Funky Broadway"	
55381	"I Get The Sweetest Feeling"/"Nothing But Heartaches"	
55392	"For Once In My Life"/"You Brought About A Change In Me"	
55402	"I Still Love You"/"Hum De Dum De Do"	1969
55418	"Helpless"/"Do It The Right Way"	

Sam Cooke

The late Sam Cooke brought his gospel-derived, pleasant singing ability to such easygoing 50's hits as "You Send Me," a 1957 classic, and to the rollicking "Everybody Likes To Cha Cha Cha." This early Keen label material by Sam Cooke was diverting but had little substance. Cooke's single releases for RCA took on a solid rhythm and blues feel. His strongest 60's material included the gospel-tinged "Bring It On Home To Me" in 1962, the blues ballad "Send Me Some Lovin'" (a Little Richard original) in 1963 and the vibrating rocker, "Shake" in 1964. The style of Sam Cooke in these and other early 60's releases influenced the sophisticated yet deeply felt soul music of later artists, in particular, Johnnie Taylor, Joe Simon and the flawless Al Greene.

Single Releases

Specialty

596	"Lovable"/"Forever" (as by Dale Cooke)	1957
619	"I'll Come Running Back To You"/"Forever"	
627	"I Don't Want To Cry"/"That's All I Need To Know"	
667	"I Need You Now"/"Happy In Love"	

Keen

4002	"For Sentimental Reasons"/"Desire Me"	1957
4009	"You Were Made For Me"/"Lonely Island"	
4013	"You Send Me"/"Summertime"	
2005	"Stealing Kisses"/"All Of My Life"	1958
2006	"Win Your Love For Me"/"Houseboat"	
2008	"Love You Most Of All"/"Blue Moon"	
2018	"Everybody Likes To Cha Cha Cha"/"Little Things You Do"	1959
2022	"Only Sixteen"/"Let's Go Steady Again"	
2101	"Summertime Pt. 1 & 2"	
2105	"There I've Said It Again"/"One Hour Ahead Of The Posse"	
2111	"T Ain't Nobody's Bizness"/"No One"	1960
2112	"Wonderful World"/"Along The Navajo Trail"	
2117	"With You"/"I Thank God"	
2118	"So Glamorous"/"Steal Away"	
2122	"Mary Mary Lou"/"Eee Yi Ee Yi Oh"	

RCA

7701	"Teenage Sonata"/"If You Were The Only Girl"	1960
7730	"You Understand Me"/"I Belong To Your Heart"	
7783	"Chain Gang"/"I Fall In Love Every Day"	
7816	"Sad Mood"/"Love Me"	
7853	"That's It—I Quit—I'm Movin' On"/"What Do You Say"	1961
7883	"Cupid"/"Farewell My Love"	
7927	"Feel It"/"It's All Right"	
7983	"Twistin' The Night Away"/"One More Time"	1962
8036	"Bring It On Home To Me"/"Having A Party"	

8088	"Nothing Can Change This Love"/"Somebody Have Mercy"	
8129	"Send Me Some Lovin'"/"Baby Baby Baby"	1963
8164	"Another Saturday Night"/"Love Will Find A Way"	
8215	"Cool Train"/"Frankie And Johnny"	
8247	"Little Red Rooster"/"You Gotta Move"	
8299	"Good News"/"Basin Street Blues"	1964
8368	"Good Times"/"Tennessee Waltz"	
8426	"Cousin Of Mine"/"That's Where It's At"	
8486	"Shake"/"A Change Is Gonna Come"	1965
8539	"Ease My Troublin' Mind"/"It's Got The Whole World Shakin'"	
8586	"When A Boy Falls In Love"/"The Piper"	
8631	"Sugar Dumpling"/"Bridge Of Tears"	
8751	"Feel It"/"That's All"	1966
8803	"Trouble Blues"/"Let's Go Steady Again"	

NOTABLE EARLY 60'S RHYTHM AND BLUES ARTISTS

Ben E. King ,

Ben E. King, lead singer with The Drifters of the late 50's, recorded several slickly written and produced singles. His most successful songs were the arrestingly poignant "Spanish Harlem," the shuffle-rhythm "Stand By Me"—an early Phil Spector production—and the emotional "I (Who Have Nothing)."

Single Releases

Atlantic
| 2067 | "A Help Each Other Romance"/"How Often" (with La Vern Baker) | 1960 |

Atco
| 6166 | "Brace Yourself"/"Show Me The Way" | 1960 |

6185	"Spanish Harlem"/"First Taste Of Love"	
6194	"Stand By Me"/"On The Horizon"	1961
6203	"Amor"/"Souvenir Of Mexico"	
6207	"Here Comes The Night"/"Young Boy Blues"	
6215	"Yes"/"Ecstasy"	
6222	"Don't Play That Song"/"The Hermit Of Misty Mountain"	1962
6231	"Too Bad"/"My Heart Cries For You"	
6237	"I'm Standing By"/"Walking In The Footsteps Of A Fool"	
6246	"Tell Daddy"/"Auf Weidersehn, My Dear"	
6256	"Gloria Gloria"/"How Can I Forget"	1963
6267	"I (Who Have Nothing)"/"The Beginning Of Time"	
6275	"I Could Have Danced All Night"/"Gypsy"	
6284	"Groovin' "/"What Now My Love"	
6288	"That's When It Hurts"/"A Man Without A Dream"	

Freddie Scott

Freddie Scott lent his powerful vocal style to the ballad hit "Hey Girl" and to the exciting, deeply felt "Are You Lonely For Me" and "You Got What I Need."

Single Releases

Arrow
724	"Please Call"	1960
726	"A Faded Memory"	

Bow
307	"Tell Them For Me"/"Hold My Hand"	1960

Joy
250	"Lost The Right"/"Baby You're A Long Time Dead"	1961
280	"I Gotta Stand Tall"/"When The Wind Changes"	1962

Colpix
692	"Hey Girl"/"The Slide"	1963
709	"I Got A Woman"/"Brand New World"	
724	"Where Does Love Go"/"Where Have All The Flowers Gone"	

Columbia
43112	"Mr. Heartache"/"One Heartache Too Many"	1964
43199	"Lonely Man"/"I'll Try Again"	1965
43316	"Come Up Singing"/"Don't Let It End"	
43623	"Forget Me If You Can"/"Little Iddy Biddy Needle"	1966

Shout
207	"Are You Lonely For Me"/"Where Were You"	
211	"Cry To Me"/"No One Could Ever Love You"	1967
212	"Am I Grooving You"/"Never You Mind"	
216	"He Will Break Your Heart"/"I'll Be Gone"	
220	"He Ain't Give You None"/"Run Joe"	
227	"Just Like A Flower"/"Spanish Harlem"	1968
233	"You Got What I Need"/"Powerful Love"	
238	"Loving You Is Killing Me"	

Elephant V Ltd.
1	"Sugar On Sunday"/"Johnny's Hill"	1969

Al Greene

Al Greene achieved soul superstardom in the early 70's. Greene's first 1967 single release was the delicately shaded "Back Up Train."

Single Releases

Hot Line Music Journal
15000	"Back Up Train"/"Don't Leave Me"	1967
15001	"Don't Hurt Me No More"/"Get Yourself Together"	1968

15002 "A Lover's Hideaway"

Hi

2164 "One Woman" 1969
2174 "You Say It"
2182 "I Can't Get Next To You"/"Ride Sally Ride"
2188 "Driving Wheel"/"True Love"

EARLY 60'S RHYTHM AND BLUES GROUPS
•

Several early 60's vocal groups can be traced to the very early and mid-50's. These rhythm and blues groups include The Drifters, Little Anthony and The Imperials, Frankie Valli and The Four Seasons, The Isley Brothers, The Olympics and The Vibrations. Each of these groups achieved solid success with their developing 60's rhythm and blues styles.

The Drifters

One of the few giant rhythm and blues groups of the 50's, The Drifters broke into the 60's with several exceptional top-40 hits. "This Magic Moment" was a sleekly performed recording that used strings with unusual effectiveness. "Save The Last Dance For Me," a much bigger hit, combined marvelous lyrics with professional arrangements and vocal work. Heavy instrumentation and forceful lyrics were used in several memorable Drifters' hits: "Up On The Roof"—a Carole King composition—in 1962, "On Broadway" in 1963 and "Under The Boardwalk" in 1964.

These major hits contributed to an early acceptance of rhythm and blues in the pop market and to the evolution of soul music during the mid and late 60's, but The Drifters never came up with a post-1964 hit. With the mid-60's success of Motown soul music, the popularity of the rhythm and blues sound of The Drifters declined. Even so, The Drifters had successfully adapted, without sacrificing emotional or artistic impact, a basic rhythm and blues sound from the 50's into a more-polished sound in the 60's.

Single Releases

As by Clyde McPhatter and The Drifters:

Atlantic
1006	"Money Honey"/"The Way I Feel"	1953
1019	"Such A Night"/"Lucille"	
1029	"Honey Love"/"Warm Your Heart"	1954
1043	"Bip Bam"/"Someday You'll Want Me To Want You"	
1048	"White Christmas"/"The Bells Of St. Mary's"	
1055	"Gone"/"What'cha Gonna Do"	1955

As by The Drifters:

Atlantic
1078	"Adorable"/"Steamboat"	1955
1089	"Ruby Baby"/"Your Promise To Be Mine"	
1101	"Soldier Of Fortune"/"I Got To Get Myself A Woman"	1956
1123	"It Was a Tear"/"Fools Fall In Love"	
1141	"Hypnotized"/"Drifting Away From You"	1957
1161	"I Know"/"Yodee Yakee"	
1187	"Drip Drop"/"Moonlight Bay"	1958
2025	"There Goes My Baby"/"Oh My Love"	1959
2040	"Dance With Me"/"True Love, True Love"	
2050	"This Magic Moment"/"Baltimore"	1960
2062	"Lonely Winds"/"Hey Señorita"	
2071	"Save The Last Dance For Me"/"Nobody But Me"	
2087	"I Count The Tears"/"Suddenly There's A Valley"	1961
2096	"Some Kind Of Wonderful"/"Honey Bee"	

2105   "Please Stay"/"No Sweet Lovin' "
2117   "Sweets For My Sweet"/"Loneliness Or
         Happiness"
2127   "Room Full Of Tears"/"Somebody New
         Dancin' With You"
2134   "When My Little Girl Is Smiling"/"Mexican   1962
         Divorce"
2143   "Stranger On The Shore"/"What To Do"
2151   "Sometimes I Wonder"/"Jackpot"
2162   "Up On The Roof"/"Another Night With The
         Boys"
2182   "On Broadway"/"Let The Music Play"   1963
2191   "Rat Race"/"If You Don't Come Back"
2201   "I'll Take You Home"/"I Feel Good All
         Over"
2216   "Vaya Con Dios"/"In The Land Of Make   1964
         Believe"
2225   "One Way Love"/"Didn't It"
2237   "Under The Boardwalk"/"I Don't Want To
         Go On Without You"
2253   "I've Got Sand In My Shoes"/"He's Just A
         Playboy"
2260   "Saturday Night At The Movies"/"Spanish
         Lace"
2261   "The Christmas Song"/"I Remember
         Christmas"
2268   "At The Club"/"Answer The Phone"   1965
2285   "Chains Of Love"/"Come On Over To My
         Place"
2292   "Follow Me"/"The Outside World"
2298   "I'll Take You Where The Music's Playing"/
         "Far From The Maddening Crowd"
2310   "We Gotta Sing"/"Nylon Stockings"
2325   "Memories Are Made Of This"/"My Islands   1966
         In The Sun"
2336   "Up In The Streets Of Harlem"/"You Can't
         Love Them All"
2366   "Baby What I Mean"/"Aretha"
2426   "Ain't It The Truth"/"Up Jumped The Devil" 1967

2471   "Still Burning In My Heart"/"I Need You
        Now"
2624   "Steal Away"/"Your Best Friend"   1969

Little Anthony and the Imperials

Known originally as The Duponts, then as The Chesters, Little Anthony and The Imperials recorded some outstanding 50's love ballads. Featuring fine lead vocal work
from the tension-packed teenage voice of Little Anthony
Guardine, "Tears On My Pillow" and the flip "Two People
In The World" are powerful romantic rhythm and blues
classics. In the early 60's, Little Anthony and The Imperials recorded several slickly produced, yet intensely emotional singles, "Goin' Out Of My Head" and "Hurt So
Bad." By the latter half of the 60's, the group was recording more middle-of-the-road material, but in 1969 they
returned to rhythm and blues with the classic "Out Of
Sight Out Of Mind and "10 Commandments Of Love."
Over the years, Little Anthony and The Imperials
recorded an impressive string of first-rate, good-selling
love ballads.

Single Releases

As by The Duponts:

Winley
    212   "You"/"Must Be Falling In Love"   1955

Royal Roost
    627   "Prove It Tonight"/"Somebody"

As by The Chesters:

Apollo
    521   "The Fires Burn No More"/"Lift Up Your   1957
           Head"

As by The Imperials:

End
  1027   "Tears On My Pillow"/"Two People In The   1958
         World"

As by Little Anthony and The Imperials:

End
  1036   "So Much"/"Oh Yeah"
  1038   "The Diary"/"Cha Cha Henry"
  1039   "Wishful Thinking"/"When You Wish Upon
         A Star"
  1047   "A Prayer And a Juke Box"/"River Path"   1959
  1053   "So Near And Yet So Far"/"I'm Alright"
  1060   "Shimmy Shimmy Ko-Ko Bop"/"I'm Still In
         Love With You"
  1067   "My Empty Room"/"Bayou Bayou Baby"   1960
  1074   "I'm Taking A Vacation From Love"/"Only
         Sympathy"
  1080   "Limbo Pt. 1 & 2"
  1083   "Formula Of Love"/"Dream"
  1086   "Please Say You Want Me"/"So Near And Yet
         So Far"
  1091   "Traveling Stranger"/"Say Yeah"
  1104   "A Lovely Way To Spend An Evening"/
         "Dream"

Roulette
  4379   "That Lil' Ole Lovemaker Me"/"It Just Ain't   1963
         Fair"
  4477   "Lonesome Romeo"/"I've Got A Lot To Offer   1964
         Darling"

DCP
  1104   "I'm On The Outside"/"Please Go"   1964
  1119   "Goin' Out Of My Head"/"Make It Easy On
         Yourself"
  1128   "Hurt So Bad"/"Reputation"   1965
  1136   "Take Me Back"/"Our Song"

1149 "I Miss You So"/"Get Out Of My Life"
1154 "Hurt"/"Never Again"   1966

Veep

1228 "Better Use Your Head"/"The Wonder Of It   1966
      All"
1233 "You Better Take It Easy Baby"/"Gonna Fix
      You Good"
1241 "Goin' Out Of My Head"/"Make It Easy On
      Yourself"

As by Anthony and The Imperials:

Veep

1248 "It's Not The Same"/"Down On Love"   1967
1255 "Don't Tie Me Down"/"Where There's A Will"
1262 "Hold On To Someone"/"Lost In Love"
1269 "You Only Live Twice"/"My Love Is A
      Rainbow"
1275 "Beautiful People"/"If I Remember To
      Forget"
1278 "I'm Hypnotized"/"Hungry Heart"   1968
1283 "What Greater Love"/"In The Back Of My
      Heart"
1293 "Gentle Rain"/"The Flesh Failures"
1303 "Anthem"/"Goodbye Goodtimes"

United Artists

50552 "Out Of Sight, Out Of Mind"/"Summer's   1969
       Comin' In"
50598 "The 10 Commandments Of Love"/"Let The
       Sun Shine In"
50625 "It'll Never Be The Same Again"/"Don't Get
       Close"
50677 "World Of Darkness"/"The Change"

The Four Seasons

Originally billed as The Four Lovers, this superb New
York group first recorded such rhythm and blues material

as the Drifters' "Honey Love" and Fats Domino's "Please Don't Leave Me." This early material was rendered with a fine rhythm and blues harmony that predated similar approaches by Dion and The Belmonts, The Passions and other East Coast white "do-wop" vocal groups. Frankie Valli then recorded "Come Si Bella" with The Romans, a poor-selling single that is now quite rare.

With the release of "Bermuda" on the Gone label, the group became The Four Seasons. The group had by then adapted to a lighter, "pop" sound which proved instantly successful in 1962 with the Vee Jay label hit, "Sherry." Sung in a crisp, high-voiced lead, "Sherry" and the follow-up "Big Girls Don't Cry" became two of the very best-selling singles at the early part of the decade. During the mid-60's, The Four Seasons maintained their popularity with "Dawn" and "Rag Doll," both sung in the engaging brisk style of "Sherry."

Single Releases

As by The Four Lovers:

RCA

6518	"The Girl In My Dreams"/"You're The Apple Of My Eye"	1956
6519	"Honey Love"/"Please Don't Leave Me"	
6646	"Be Lovey Dovey"/"Jambalaya"	
6768	"Happy Am I"/"Never Never"	
6819	"The Stranger"/"Night Train"	1957

As by Frankie Valli and The Romans:

Cindy

3012	"Come Si Bella"/"Real"	1958

As by The Four Seasons:

Gone

5122	"Bermuda"/"Spanish Lace"	1960

Alanna
   555 "Don't Sweat It Baby"/"That's The Way The
          Ball Bounces"

Vee Jay
   456 "Sherry"/"I've Cried Before"   1962
   465 "Big Girls Don't Cry"/"Connie O"
   478 "Santa Claus Is Coming To Town"/
          "Christmas Tears"
   485 "Walk Like A Man"/"Lucky Ladybug"   1963
   512 "Ain't That A Shame"/"Soon"
   539 "Candy Girl"/"Marlena"
   562 "New Mexican Rose"/"That's The Only Way"
   576 "Peanuts"/"Stay"
   582 "Goodnight My Love"/"Stay"   1964
   597 "Long Lonely Nights"/"Alone"
   608 "Sincerely"/"One Song"
   618 "Happy Happy Birthday Baby"/"Apple Of
          My Eye"
   626 "I Saw Mommy Kissing Santa Claus"/
          "Christmas Tears"
   639 "Never On Sunday"/"Connie O"   1965
   664 "Tonite Tonite"
   713 "Little Boy"/"Silver Wings"
   719 "My Mother's Eyes"/"Stay"

Phillips
  40166 "Dawn"/"No Surfin' Today"   1964
  40185 "Ronnie"/"Born To Wander"
  40211 "Rag Doll"/"Silence Is Golden"
  40225 "Save It For Me"/"Funny Face"
  40238 "Big Man In Town"/"Little Angel"
  40260 "Bye Bye Baby"/"Searching Wind"   1965
  40278 "Toy Soldier"/"Betrayed"
  40305 "Girl Come Running"/"Cry Myself To Sleep"
  40317 "Let's Hang On"/"On Broadway Tonight"
  40350 "Working My Way Back To You"/"Too Many 1966
           Memories"
  40370 "Opus 17"/"Beggar's Parade"
  40393 "I've Got You Under My Skin"/"Huggin' My
           Pillow"

40412	"Tell It To The Rain"/"Show Girl"	
40433	"Beggin' "/"Dody"	1967
40460	"C'mon Marianne"/"Let's Ride Again"	
40490	"Watch The Flowers Grow"/"Raven"	
40523	"Will You Love Me Tomorrow"/"Around And Around"	1968
40542	"Saturday's Father"/"Goodbye Girl"	
40577	"Electric Stories"/"Pity"	
40597	"Idaho"/"Something's On Her Mind"	1969
40688	"Heartaches And Rain Drops"/"Lay Me Down"	
40694	"Where Are My Dreams"	

The Isley Brothers

The Isley Brothers first recorded two late 50's ballads, "The Angels Cried" and "Don't Be Jealous;" neither was a hit. They then recorded the exciting, gospel-tinged "Shout," which was not only a stone smash hit, but a consistent 60's best-seller that eventually influenced rhythm and blues throughout the decade. The Isley Brothers recorded several other screaming rockers for RCA, Atlantic and Wand, for whom they had the sizable hit, "Twist And Shout." Two years later, "Twist And Shout," essentially a rerecording of "Shout" with a twist beat, was a major Beatles hit. The Brothers then recorded more-subdued material for Tamla records, including the fine, cheerful "This Old Heart Of Mine," again a hit. In 1968, The Isley Brothers adapted the very popular "boogaloo" beat to their biggest hit ever, "It's Your Thing." The Isley Brothers were a singularly creative rhythm and blues group who helped keep music vital and interesting during the 60's.

Single Releases

Teenage
| 1004 | "Angels Cried"/"The Cow Jumped Over The Moon" | 1957 |

Cindy
3009 "Don't Be Jealous"/"This Is The End"   1958

Gone
5022 "I Wanna Know"/"Everybody's Gonna Rock   1959
     And Roll"
5048 "My Love"/"The Drag"

Mark X
8000 "Rockin' MacDonald"/"The Drag"

RCA
7588 "Shout Pt. 1 & 2"   1959
     (rereleased in 1962)
7657 "Respectable"/"Without A Song"
7718 "How Deep Is The Ocean"/"He's Got The
     Whole World In His Hands"
7746 "Open Up Your Heart"/"Gypsy Love Song"   1960
7787 "Tell Me Who"/"Say You Love Me Too"

Atlantic
2092 "Teach Me How To Shimmy"/"Jeepers   1960
     Creepers"
2100 "Standing On The Dance Floor"/"Shine On   1961
     Harvest Moon"
2110 "Your Old Lady"/"Write To Me"
2122 "A Fool For You"/"Just One More Time"

Wand
118 "Right Now"/"The Snake"   1961
124 "Twist And Shout"/"Spanish Twist"   1962
127 "Twistin' With Linda"/"You Better Come
    Home"
131 "Nobody But Me"/"I'm Laughing To Keep
    From Crying"
137 "Hold On Baby"/"I Say Love"

United Artists
605 "Tango"/"She's Gone"   1963
659 "Please Please Please"/"You'll Never Leave
    Him"
714 "Who's That Lady"/"My Little Girl"

Atlantic
2263	"The Last Girl"/"Lookin' For A Love"	1964
2277	"Wild As A Tiger"/"Simon Says"	
2303	"Move Over And Let Me Dance"/"Have You Ever Been Disappointed"	

T Neck
| 501 | "Testify Pt. 1 & 2" | 1964 |

Tamla
54128	"This Old Heart Of Mine"/"There's No Love Left"	1966
54133	"Take Some Time Out For Love"/"Who Could Ever Doubt My Love"	
54135	"I Guess I'll Always Love You"/"I Hear A Symphony"	
54146	"Got To Have You Back"/"Just Ain't Enough Love"	1967
54154	"That's The Way Love Is"/"One Too Many Heartaches"	
54164	"Take Me In Your Arms"/"Why When Love Is Gone"	1968
54175	"All Because I Love You"/"Behind A Painted Smile"	
54182	"Just Ain't Enough Love"/"Take Some Time Out For Love"	1969

T Neck
901	"It's Your Thing"/"Don't Give It Away"	1968
902	"I Turned You On"/"I Know Who You've Been Socking It To"	1969
906	"Black Berries Pt. 1 & 2"	
908	"Was It Good To You"/"I Got To Get Myself Together"	
912	"Give The Women What They Want"/"Bless Your Heart"	

The Olympics

From their initial classic hit, "Western Movies," The Olympics specialized in wild stomping rock and roll. The piano-pounder "Big Boy Pete" was a hit well into the 60's, as was the earlier "Hully Gully." Into the mid-60's The Olympics recorded a long series of rock and roll dances: "The Chicken" in 1961, the rhythmic "Bounce" in 1963 and "Baby, Do The Philly Dog" in 1966. Other hits were the engaging "Good Lovin'" and "Mine Exclusively." The Olympics were unsurpassed in frantic flat-out rock and roll performances.

Single Releases

Demon
1508	"Western Movies"/"Well"	1958
1512	"Dance With The Teacher"/"Ev'rybody Needs Love"	
1514	"Chicken"/"Your Love"	

Arvee
562	"Hully Gully"/"Private Eye"	1959
595	"Big Boy Pete"/"The Slop"	
5006	"Shimmy Like Kate"/"Workin' Hard"	1960
5020	"Dance By The Light Of The Moon"/"Dodge City"	
5023	"Little Pedro"/"Bull Fight" (by Cappy Lewis)	1961
5031	"Dooley"/"Stay Where You Are"	
5044	"The Stomp"/"Mash Them 'Taters'"	
5051	"Twist"/"Everybody Likes To Cha Cha Cha"	1962
5056	"The Scotch"/"Baby It's Hot"	
5073	"What'd I Say Pt. 1 & 2"	
6501	"Big Boy Pete '65"/"Stay Where You Are"	1965

Titan
1718	"Chicken"/"Cool Short"	1961

Duo Disc
104	"The Boogler Pt. 1 & 2"	1962

Tri Disc
106	"The Bounce"/"Fireworks"	1963
107	"Dancin' Holiday"/"Do The Slauson Shuffle"	

110　"Bounce Again"/"A New Dancin' Partner"
112　"The Broken Hip"/"So Goodbye"

Loma
2010　"I'm Comin' Home"/"Rainin' In My Heart"　　1964
2013　"Good Lovin'"/"Olympic Shuffle"　　1965
2017　"Baby I'm Yours"/"No More Will I Cry"

Warner Bros.
7369　"Please Please Please"/"Girl, You're My Kind　1965
　　　Of People"

Mirwood
5504　"We Go Together"/"Secret Agents"　　1965
5513　"Mine Exclusively"/"Secret Agents"　　1966
5523　"Baby, Do The Philly Dog"/"Western Movies"
5525　"The Duck"/"The Bounce"
5529　"I'll Do A Little Bit More"/"The Same Old　1967
　　　Thing"

Parkway
6003　"Lookin' For A Love"/"Good Things"　　1968

The Vibrations

As The Jayhawks, the group introduced the 50's classic, "Stranded In The Jungle." During the 60's, The Vibrations recorded the quick-tempo dance "The Watusi," a guitar-backed rock and roll gem. In 1961, The Vibrations issued a "Hully Gully" parody entitled "Peanut Butter" as by The Marathons for the Arvee label. This recording was issued on Argo by The Vibrations apparently in partial settlement of a contract dispute—the label reads: "Vibrations named by others as Marathons," the latter group name in prominent type. In 1964, The Vibrations moved to the Atlantic label, on which they recorded a rambling-beat hit, "My Girl Sloopy." The Vibrations had a long series of unspectacular Okeh label releases, but they didn't come up with a post-1964 hit.

Single Releases

As by The Jayhawks:

Flash

105	"Counting My Teardrops"/"The Devil's Cousin"	1956
109	"Stranded In The Jungle"/"My Only Darling"	
111	"Love Train"/"Don't Mind Dyin'"	

Aladdin

3393	"The Creature"/"Everyone Should Know"	1957

Eastman

792	"Start The Fire"/"I Wish The World Owed Me A Living"	1957

As by The Vibrations:

Bet

001	"So Blue"/"Love Me Like You Should" (also on Checker 954)	1959

Checker

961	"Feel So Bad"/"Cave Man"	1959
969	"The Watusi"/"Wallflower"	
974	"Continental With Me Baby"/"The Junkeroo"	1960
982	"Stranded In The Jungle"/"Don't Say Goodbye"	
987	"All My Love Belongs To You"/"Stop Right Now"	1961
990	"Let's Pony Again"/"What Made You Change Your Mind"	
1002	"Oh Cindy"/"Over The Rainbow"	1962
1011	"The New Hully Gully"/"Anytime"	
1022	"If He Don't"/"Hamburgers On A Bun"	1963
1038	"Since I Fell For You"/"May The Best Man Win"	
1061	"Dancing Danny"	1964

As by The Marathons:

Arvee
5027   "Peanut Butter"/"Talkin' Trash"   1961

As by The Vibrations:

Argo
5389   "Peanut Butter"/"Down In New Orleans"   1961

Atlantic
2204   "Between Hello And Goodbye"/"Lonesome   1964
        Little Lonely Girl"
2221   "My Girl Sloopy"/"Daddy Woo-Woo"

Okeh
7205   "Sloop Dance"/"Watusi Time"   1964
7212   "Hello Happiness"/"Keep On Keeping On"
7220   "End Up Crying"/"Ain't Love That Way"   1965
7228   "If I Only Knew"/"Talkin' Bout Love"
7230   "Misty"/"Finding Out The Hard Way"
7241   "Canadian Sunset"/"The Story Of A Starry   1966
        Night"
7249   "Gonna Get Along Without You Now"/
        "Forgive And Forget"
7257   "And I Love Her"/"Soul A Go-Go"
7276   "Pick Me"/"You Better Beware"   1967
7297   "Come To Yourself"/"Together"
7311   "Love In Them There Hills"/"Remember The   1968
        Rain"

Epic
10418   "Cause You're Mine"/"I Took An Overdose"   1968

Amy
11006   "A Shot Of Love"   1968

Neptune
19   "Expressway To Your Heart"/"Who's Gonna   1969
        Help Me Now"
20   "Smoke Signals"/"Who's Gonna Help Me
        Now"

NOTABLE "DO-WOP" VOCAL GROUPS

Several rhythm and blues vocal groups that originated in the very early 60's effectively captured the romantic ballad sound clearly derived from 50's rhythm and blues vocal styles.

The Passions

The Passions were an early white vocal group who featured a style drawn from Dion and The Belmonts and other New York vocal groups. The love song "Just To Be With You" was a sizable 1959–1960 hit. The 1960 version of "Gloria" was an exceptional rendition of the Cadillacs' original (Josie 765). Although The Passions were a consistently fine ballad group, they didn't have any post-1960 hits.

Single Releases

Audicon
102	"Just To Be With You"/"Oh Melancholy Me"	1959
105	"I Only Want You"/"This Is My Love"	
106	"Gloria"/"Jungle Drums"	1960
108	"Beautiful Dreamer"/"One Look Is All It Took"	
112	"Made For Lovers"/"You Don't Love Me Anymore"	

Diamond
146	"Sixteen Candles"/"The Third Floor"	1960

Unique
79	"Too Many Memories"/"The Reason"	1961

Octavia
8005	"I Gotta Know"/"Aphrodite"	1961

Jubilee
5406	"Lonely Road"/"One Look Is All It Took"	1962

ABC
10436   "The Bully"/"Empty Seat"

The Van Dykes

The Van Dykes never had a major hit, yet their "No Man Is An Island" is one of the better rhythm and blues releases of the decade, an unusual blend of memorable lyrics with a mellow, delicate vocal performance.

Single Releases

Donna
1333   "Gift Of Love"/"Guardian Angel"   1960

King
5158   "The Bells Are Ringing"/"Meaning Of Love"   1961
          (also on DeLuxe 6193)

Atlantic
2161   "King Of Fools"/"Stupidity"   1962

Mala
520   "No Man Is An Island"/"I Won't Hold It   1965
          Against You"
530   "I've Got To Go On Without You"/"What Will   1966
          I Do"
539   "Never Let Me Go"/"I've Got To Find A
          Love"
549   "You Need Confidence"/"You're Shakin' Me
          Up"
566   "A Sunday Kind Of Love"/"I'm So Happy"   1967
584   "Tears Of Joy"/"Save My Love For A Rainy
          Day"

The Marcels

The Marcels, a Pittsburgh group in the racially mixed tradition of The Dell Vikings, had the major hit of 1961, the infectious "Blue Moon." "Blue Moon" stood out because of the classic "bomp bomp" assistance of the bass singer, a device faithfully borrowed from 50's rhythm and blues. This same gimmick enhanced the follow-up standards "Summertime," "My Melancholy Baby" and "Heartaches."

Single Releases

Colpix

186	"Blue Moon"/"Goodbye To Love"	1961
196	"Summertime"/"Teeter Totter Love"	
606	"You Are My Sunshine"/"Find Another Fool"	
612	"Heartaches"/"My Love For You"	
617	"Merry Twist-Max"/"Don't Cry For Me This Christmas"	
624	"My Melancholy Baby"/"Really Need Your Love"	1962
629	"Footprints In The Sand"/"Twistin' Fever"	
640	"Flowerpot"/"Lollipop Baby"	
651	"Friendly Loans"/"Loved Her The Whole Week Through"	
665	"All-Right—OK You Win"	
683	"That Old Black Magic"/"Don't Turn Your Back On Me"	
694	"One Last Kiss"/"You Got To Be Sincere"	1963

Shep and The Limelites

Shep and The Limelites were drawn from the 50's Heartbeats vocal group. Lead singer James Shepherd was also lead of The Heartbeats, answering his own Heartbeats' "A Thousand Miles Away" (Hull 720/Rama 216) with "Daddy's Home." This smash hit coincided with a 1961–1962 50's revival. During this minirevival such records as "In The Still of The Nite" by The Five Satins (Ember 1005), "Baby Oh Baby" by The Shells (Johnson 104) and "The Closer You Are" by The Channels (Whirlin' Disc 100) again received chart action. This was the first of several 50's rebirths during the decade. Follow-up releases by Shep and The Limelites remained faithful to the 50's love song mold, especially in their fine "Our Anniversary."

Single Releases

Hull

740	"Daddy's Home"/"This I Know"	1961
742	"Ready For Love"/"You'll Be Sorry"	
747	"Three Steps From The Altar"/"Oh What A Feeling"	1962
748	"Our Anniversary"/"Who Told The Sandman"	
751	"What Did Daddy Do"/"Teach Me How To Twist"	
753	"Everything Is Gonna Be Alright"/"Gee Baby What About You"	1963
756	"Remember Baby"/"The Monkey"	
757	"Stick By Me"/"It's All Over Now"	1964
759	"Steal Away"/"For You My Love"	
761	"Why Won't You Believe Me"/"Easy To Remember"	
767	"Why Did You Fall For Me"/"I'm All Alone"	1965
770	"Party For Two"/"You Better Believe"	
772	"I'm A Hurtin' Inside"/"In Case I Forget"	

The Jive Five

The Jive Five had a smash hit with "My True Story," a high-voice, pleading performance. This style was also effective in "Never Never" and "What Time Is It." The Jive Five maintained moderate popularity throughout the 60's, in the later 60's choosing to record contemporary soul material.

Single Releases

Beltone
1006	"My True Story"/"When I Was Single"	1961
1014	"Never Never"/"People From Another World"	
2019	"No Not Again"/"Hully Gully Callin' Time"	1962
2024	"What Time Is It"/"Beggin' You Please"	
2029	"These Golden Rings"/"Do You Hear Wedding Bells"	
2030	"Johnny Never Knew"/"Lili Marlene"	1963
2034	"Rain"/"She's My Girl"	

Sketch
219	"United"/"Prove Every Word You Say" (also on United Artists 807)	1964

United Artists
853	"I'm A Happy Man"/"Kiss Kiss Kiss"	1965
936	"A Bench In The Park"/"Please Baby Please"	
50004	"Goin' Wild"/"Main Street"	1966
50033	"In My Neighborhood"/"Then Came Heartbreak"	
50069	"You're A Puzzle"/"Ha Ha"	
50107	"You Promised Me Great Things"/"You"	

Musicor
1250	"Crying Like A Baby"/"You'll Fall In Love"	1967
1270	"No More Tears"/"You'll Fall In Love"	
1305	"Sugar"/"Blues In The Ghetto"	1968

Avco
4568	"Come Down In Time"	1968

The Manhattans

The Manhattans, a relatively unknown yet consistently professional ballad group, hit well with "Baby I Need You." The group continues recording fine, soulful harmony.

Single Releases

504	"Ive Got Everything But You"/"For The Very First Time"	1962
506	"There Goes A Fool"/"Call Somebody Please"	
507	"I Wanna Be"/"What's It Gonna Be"	
509	"Searching For My Baby"/"I'm The One That Love Forgot"	1964
512	"Follow Your Heart"/"The Boston Monkey"	1965
514	"Baby I Need You"/"Teach Me"	1966
517	"Can I"/"That New Girl"	
522	"I Bet 'Cha"/"Sweet Little Girl"	
524	"Alone On New Year's Eve"/"It's That Time Of The Year"	
526	"Our Love Will Never Die"/"All I Need Is Your Love"	1967
529	"When We're Made As One"/"Baby I'm Sorry"	
533	"I Call It Love"/"Manhattan Stomp"	
542	"I Don't Wanna Go"/"Love Is Breaking Out"	1969

DeLuxe

115	"It's Gonna Take A Lot"/"Give Him Up"	1969
132	"Let Them Talk Pt. 1 & 2"	
139	"One Life To Live"/"It's The Only Way"	

The Shirelles

The early 60's was a period of unprecedented popularity for female rhythm and blues vocal groups. The very successful Shirelles were largely responsible for this trend. They recorded in a slickly produced, tightly harmonious style, which became the basic approach of a dozen or so other female groups that drew from The Shirelles.

The Decca label singles were mild-selling records. "I Met Him On A Sunday" was an excellent pop-flavored up-tempo release; "Dedicated To The One I Love," a remake of The Five Royales' original (King 5098), was rendered in a pleading fashion and didn't become a major hit until fully one year after its 1959 release date. "Tonight's The Night"—the first 60's hit by The Shirelles— "(Will You Love Me) Tomorrow" and "Mama Said" were each performed in the engaging "I Met Him On A Sunday" style. All were major hits. An outstanding later hit was the sympathetically phrased "Soldier Boy," a beautiful ballad release. By the mid-60's, the skyrocketing Supremes and other soul music groups had eclipsed the Shirelles, but their numerous accessible, rhythmic recordings had already made them a major and influential 60's vocal group.

Single Releases

Decca
30588	"I Met Him On A Sunday"/"I Want You To Be My Boyfriend"	1958
30669	"My Love Is A Charm"/"Slop Time"	
30761	"I Got The Message"/"Stop Me"	

Scepter
1203	"Dedicated To The One I Love"/"Look A Here Baby"	1959
1205	"Doin' The Ronde"/"A Teardrop And A Lollipop"	
1208	"Tonight's The Night"/"The Dance Is Over"	1960
1211	"(Will You Love Me) Tomorrow"/"Boys"	
1217	"Mama Said"/"Blue Holiday"	1961
1220	"What A Sweet Thing That Was"/"A Thing Of The Past"	
1223	"Big John"/"21"	
1227	"Baby It's You"/"The Things I Want To Hear"	
1228	"Soldier Boy"/"Love Is A Swingin' Thing"	1962
1234	"Welcome Home Baby"/"Mama, Here Comes The Bride"	
1237	"It's Love That Really Counts"/"Stop The Music"	

The Orlons

The Orlons were an early Philadelphia female vocal group influenced by the brisk upbeat Shirelles' recordings, but a bit more aggressive in approach. "The Wah-Watusi" along with "Don't Hang Up," "South Street" and "Not Me" were very successful hits. "Rules Of Love," The Orlons' final hit, was an exciting, shouting group effort.

Single Releases

Cameo

295	"Shimmy Shimmy"/"Everything Nice"	1964
319	"Rules Of Love"/"Heartbreak Hotel"	
332	"Goin' Places"/"Knock Knock Who's There"	
352	"Come On Down Baby Baby"/"I Ain't Comin' Back"	
372	"Don't You Want My Lovin' "/"I Can't Take It"	1965
384	"No Love But Your Love"/"Envy"	

NOTABLE FEMALE VOCAL GROUPS

The Chiffons

Several notable early 60's female vocal groups drew heavily from various sources—the happy infectious style of The Shirelles and The Orlons and the lush creations of Phil Spector's Philles label vocal groups. The Chiffons were among the earliest of these groups, socking out "He's So Fine" and two successful follow-up hits.

Single Releases

Big Deal
| 6003 | "Tonight's The Night"/"Do You Know" | 1960 |

Laurie
3152	"He's So Fine"/"Oh My Lover"	1962
3166	"Why Am I So Shy"/"Lucky Me"	
3179	"One Fine Day"/"Why Am I So Shy"	1963
3195	"A Love So Fine"/"Only My Friend"	
3212	"I Have A Boyfriend"/"I'm Gonna Dry My Eyes"	
3224	"Tonight I Met An Angel"/"Easy To Love"	
3262	"Sailor Boy"	
3301	"The Real Thing"/"Nobody Knows What's Goin On"	
3340	"Sweet Talkin' Guy"/"Did You Ever Go Steady"	

3364   "My Boyfriend's Back"/"I Got Plenty O
Nuttin' "

The Cookies

The Cookies performed some of Carole King's fine
material, including the rolling-tempo "Chains" and "Don't
Say Nothing Bad."

Single Releases

Dimension
1002   "Chains"/"Stranger In My Arms"   1962
1008   "Don't Say Nothin' Bad"/"Softly In The   1963
Night"
1012   "Will Power"/"I Want A Boy For My
Birthday"

The Exciters

The Exciters were a rapid-fire dance-beat vocal group.
Their major hit was "Tell Him."

Single Releases

United Artists
544   "Tell Him"/"Hard Way To Go"   1962
572   "He's Got The Power"/"Drama Of Love"
662   "Do-Wah-Diddy"/"If Love Came Your Way"   1963
664   "Get Him"/"It's So Exciting"

The Shangri-Las

The Shangri-Las, the most successful Red Bird label
group (a New York equivalent of the Philles label "Spec-

tor Sound"), had several major hits. Their most successful singles were the hauntingly passionate "Remember (Walkin' In The Sand)" and the dramatic "Leader Of The Pack"—strikingly similar to The Crystals' "He's A Rebel."

Single Releases

Red Bird

10008	"Remember (Walkin' In The Sand)"/"Give Us Your Blessing"	1964
10014	"Leader Of The Pack"/"I Can Never Go Home Anymore"	
10018	"Give Him A Great Big Kiss"/"Twist And Shout"	1965
10019	"Maybe"/"Shout"	
10025	"Out In The Streets"/"The Boy"	
10030	"Heaven Only Knows"/"Give Us Your Blessing"	
10043	"I Can Never Go Home Anymore"/"Bull Dog"	
10048	"Sophisticated"/"Boom Boom"	
10068	"Paradise"/"Past Present & Future"	

The Dixie Cups

The Dixie Cups, also a Red Bird group, had two pleasant, lightweight hits, "Chapel Of Love" and "Iko Iko."

Single Releases

Red Bird

10001	"Chapel Of Love"/"Ain't That Nice"	1964
10006	"People Say"/"Girls Can Tell"	
10012	"You Should Have Seen The Way He Looked At Me"/"No True Love"	
10017	"Little Bell"	1965
10024	"Iko Iko"/"Gee Baby Gee"	

The Jewels

The Jewels had a solitary hit, the bluesy "Opportunity."

Single Releases

Dimension
   1034 "Opportunity"/"Gotta Find A Way"   1964
   1048 "Smokey Joe"/"But I Do"

The Philles Sound

Philles Records—an early Phil Spector enterprise—issued some unusually fine rhythm and blues recordings. Philles releases were noted for lush background work and often referred to as "wall of sound" productions. Their highly produced backing became as prominent in the recording as the singing of the group. Harmony was not emphasized as much as the power of combined vocal energy.

The earliest successful Philles rhythm and blues vocal groups were The Crystals, The Ronettes and Bob B. Soxx and The Blue Jeans. Darlene Love had several successful releases, but Philles only became a major label with the release of later singles by The Righteous Brothers and Ike and Tina Turner.

Philles was essentially a 45 RPM label for which the single represented the total creation and was an artistic end in itself. Philles label releases were more often than not among the best rhythm and blues records of the decade. Philles tried to come up with the perfect single record— the prototype rock and roll production—and two releases, "You've Lost That Lovin' Feelin'" by The Righteous Brothers and "River Deep—Mountain High" by Ike and Tina Turner, came close.

Several of the earliest Philles releases, such as The Crystals "He Hit Me" (And It Felt Like A Kiss)," are now hard to obtain and often bring $5 or more. Collectors of Spector material seek out a complete Philles label collection—from Philles #100 to #136. These single records include several obscure releases by Joel Scott (Philles 101), Ali Hassan (Philles 103) and Steve Douglas (Philles 104), each of which can bring $5. An entire single issue collection is worth well over $100.

NOTABLE PHILLES SOUND ARTISTS

The Crystals

The Crystals favored lyrics with strong emotional impact. Among these were the grabbers, "Uptown," "He's A Rebel" and the controversial "He Hit Me (And It Felt Like A Kiss)." Two other issues, "He's Sure The Boy I Love" and "Da Doo Ron Ron," were fine rock and roll records.

Single Releases

Philles

100	"There's No Other"/"Oh Yeah Maybe Baby"	1961
102	"Uptown"/"What A Nice Way To Turn Seventeen"	1962
105	"He Hit Me (And It Felt Like A Kiss)"/"No One Ever Tells You"	
106	"He's A Rebel"/"I Love You Eddie"	
109	"He's Sure The Boy I Love"/"Walkin' Along"	
112	"Da Doo Ron Ron"/"Git 'It"	1963
115	"Then He Kissed Me"/"Brother Julius"	
119X	"Little Boy"/"Harry And Milt"	1964
122	"All Grown Up"/"Irving"	

United Artists

927	"My Place"/"You Can't Tie A Good Girl Down"	1965
994	"I Got A Man"/"Are You Trying To Get Rid Of Me Baby"	1966

The Ronettes

The Ronettes recorded two best-sellers—the fine "Be My Baby" and "Baby I Love You." Later releases featured the unusual harmony used in "Breakin' Up" or sound effects like the storm used in "Walkin' In The Rain."

Single Releases

Colpix
646   "I'm Gonna Quit While I'm Ahead"/"I'm On   1962
      The Wagon"

May
114   "You Bet I Would"
138   "Memory"/"Good Girls"

Philles
116   "Be My Baby"/"Tedesco & Pittman"   1963
118   "Baby I Love You"/"Miss Joan & Mr. Sam"
120   "Breakin' Up"/"Big Red"   1964
121   "Do I Love You"/"Bebe & Susu"
123   "Walkin' In The Rain"/"How Does It Feel"
126   "Born To Be Together"/"Blues For My Baby" 1965
128   "Oh I Love You"/"Is This What I Get For
      Loving You"
133   "I Can Hear Music"/"When I Saw You"   1966

A&M
1040 "Oh I Love You"/"You Came You Saw You
      Conquered"   1968

Bob B. Soxx and The Blue Jeans

Bob B. Soxx and The Blue Jeans' major hit was the booming arrangement of "Zip A Dee Doo Dah." The group sang "Why Do Lovers Break Each Other's Hearts" in a style strongly suggestive of The Teenagers' "Why Do Fools Fall In Love" (Gee 1012).

Single Releases

Philles

107	"Zip A Dee Doo Dah"/"Flip & Nitty"	1962
110	"Why Do Lovers Break Each Other's Hearts"/ "Dr. Kaplan's Office"	
113	"Not Too Young To Get Married"/"Annette"	1963

Darlene Love

Darlene Love was the sole successful Philles label single artist. Her biggest hit was the appealingly rendered "The Boy I'm Gonna Marry."

Single Releases

Philles

111	"The Boy I'm Gonna Marry"/"Playing For Keeps"	1962
114	"Wait Til My Bobby Gets Home"/"Take It From Me"	1963
117	"A Fine Fine Boy"/"Nino & Sonny"	
119	"Christmas Baby Please Come Home"/ "Winter Wonderland (also on Philles 125)	
123	"He's A Quiet Guy"/"Stumbled & Fell"	1964

NOTABLE RHYTHM AND BLUES VOCAL GROUPS

The O'Jays

The O'Jays, a major soul music group in the 70's, began recording in the early 60's with such upbeat blues material as "Lonely Drifter" and "Lipstick Traces"—both are contagiously rhythmic records—and with the New Orleans-influenced, down-home ballad "I've Cried My Last Tear." The gently sung "I'll Be Sweeter Tomorrow" represents their approach to a more professionally produced soul music. The O'Jays consistently sing with an emotional impact especially well communicated by the fine lyrics of "One Night Affair"—The O'Jays' first major hit.

Single Releases

Apollo

759	"Miracles"/"Can't Take It"	1960

Little Star

124	"Crack Up Laughing"/"How Does It Feel" (also on Imperial 5942)	1963

Imperial

5976	"Lonely Drifter"/"That's Enough"	1963
66007	"The Storm Is Over"/"Stand Tall"	1964
66025	"I'll Never Stop Loving You"/"My Dearest Beloved"	
66037	"Lovely Dee"/"You're On Top"	
66076	"Oh How You Hurt Me"/"Girl Machine"	
66102	"Lipstick Traces"/"Think It Over Baby"	1965
66121	"I've Cried My Last Tear"/"Whip It On Me Baby"	
66131	"Let It All Out"/"You're The One"	
66145	"It Won't Hurt"/"I'll Never Let You Go"	
66162	"Pretty Words"/"I'll Never Forget You"	
66177	"No Time For You"/"A Blowing Wind"	
66197	"Stand In For Love"/"Friday Night"	

Minit

32015	"Working On Your Case"/"Hold On"	1966

Bell

691	"I'll Be Sweeter Tomorrow"/"I Dig Your Act"	1967
704	"Look Over Your Shoulder"/"I'm So Glad I Found You"	1968
737	"Going Going Gone"/"The Choice"	
749	"I Miss You"/"Now That I Found You"	
770	"Don't You Know A True Love"/"That's Alright"	1969

Saru
    1220   "La De Da"/"Shattered Man"   1968

Neptune
      12   "One Night Affair"/"There's Someone"   1969
      18   "Branded Bad"/"You're The Best Thing Since
             Candy"
      20   "Without The One You Love"
      22   "Deeper"/"I've Got The Groove"

The Rivingtons

The Rivingtons, a group partially drawn from the 50's
Lamplighters, had success with their early staccato-tempo
rock and roll releases. Their most memorable record was
"Papa-Oom-Mow-Mow," an exceptional novelty-dance
record. Follow-up issues were performed in a similar
aggressive up-tempo style, notably the much-imitated
"The Bird's The Word." Hardly as well known were several fine ballad flip sides by The Rivingtons, such as
"Cherry," a love song complete with an absurdly drawn-
out spoken break.

Single Releases

Liberty
    55427   "Papa-Oom-Mow-Mow"/"Deep Water"   1962
    55513   "Kickapoo Joy Juice"/"My Reward"
    55528   "Mama-Oom-Mow-Mow"/"Waiting"
    55553   "The Bird's The Word"/"I'm Losing My Grip" 1963
    55585   "The Shaky Bird Pt. 1 & 2"
    55610   "Little Sally Walker"/"Cherry"
    55671   'Weejee Walk"/"Fairy Tales"

American
     100   "All That Glitters"/"You Move Me Baby"   1964
             (also on Vee Jay 634)

Reprise
   0293   "I Tried"/"One Monkey"   1964

Vee Jay
   649   "Years Of Tears"/"I Love You Always"   1964
   677   "The Willy"/"Just Got To Be Mine" (also on
       Newman 605)

Columbia
  43581   "Tend To Business"/"A Rose Growing In   1966
       The Ruins"
  43772   "Yadi-Yadi-Yum-Dum"/"Yadi Yadi Revisited"

Quan
  1379   "I Don't Want A New Baby"/"You're Gonna   1967
       Pay"

Baton Master
   202   "Teach Me Tonight"/"Reach Our Goal"   1967

RCA
  0301   "Pop Your Corn Pt. 1 & 2"   1969

Mitch Ryder and The Detroit Wheels

Mitch Ryder and The Detroit Wheels specialized in discothèque rock and roll with such challenging dance records as "Jenny Take A Ride" and the interminable "Devil With The Blue Dress On and Good Golly Miss Molly." Since Ryder often drew his material from 50's hit song medleys using a nonstop-tempo, he produced numerous "sound alike" rock and roll records.

Single Releases

New Voice
   806   "Jenny Take A Ride"/"Baby Jane"   1965
   808   "Little Latin Lupe Lu"/"I Hope"   1966
   811   "Break Out"/"I Need Help"

814   "Takin' All I Can Get"/"You Can Get Your
      Kicks"
817   "Devil With The Blue Dress On And Good
      Golly Miss Molly"/"I Had It Made"
820   "Sock It To Me Baby"/"I Never Had It   1967
      Better"
822   "Too Many Fish In The Sea And Three Little
      Fishes"/"One Grain Of Sand"
824   "Joy"/"I'd Rather Go To Jail"
826   "You Are My Sunshine"/"Wild Child"
828   "Come See About Me"/"A Face In The
      Crowd"
830   "Ruby Baby"/"Peaches On A Cherry Tree"   1968

Dyno Voice
901   "What Now My Love"/"Blessing In Disguise"   1968
905   "Personality And Chantilly Lace"/"Make A
      Fool Of Myself"
916   "The Lights Of Night"/"I Need Lovin' You"
934   "Ring Your Bell"/"Baby I Need Your Loving
      With Theme For Mitch"

The Young Rascals

The Young Rascals, later known simply as The Rascals,
had early hit success with versions of rhythm and blues
material—"Slow Down," "Good Lovin' " and "Mustang Sally"—performed in a slick rock-tempo. "Groovin' " was a
departure from this approach. "Groovin' " is a softly sung
rock and roll ballad with fine, wispy lyrics that effectively
portray the aimless mid-60's lifestyle. The Young Rascals
used this highly agreeable approach to advantage with
the mood-setting "How Can I Be Sure" and the accessible
"A Beautiful Morning."

In late 1968, The Rascals began to deal with social
awareness in the intensely sincere "People Got To Be
Free"—a fine rock and roll record and an effective "message" record as well. The Rascals continued to record at a

professional level throughout the decade. Their excellent "Carry Me Back" reflects the times in very personal musical terms.

Single Releases

As by The Young Rascals:

Atlantic

2312	"I Ain't Gonna Eat Out My Heart Anymore"/ "Slow Down"	1965
2321	"Good Lovin' "/"Mustang Sally"	1966
2338	"You Better Run"/"Love Is A Beautiful Thing"	
2353	"Come On Up"/"What Is The Reason"	
2377	"I've Been Lonely Too Long"/"If You Knew"	1967
2401	"Groovin' "/"Sueño"	
2424	"A Girl Like You"/"It's Love"	
2438	"How Can I Be Sure"/"I'm So Happy Now"	
2463	"It's Wonderful"/"Of Course"	

As by The Rascals:

Atlantic

2493	"A Beautiful Morning"/"Rainy Day"	1968
2537	"People Got To Be Free"/"My World"	
2584	"A Ray Of Hope"/"Any Dance'll Do"	1969
2599	"Heaven"/"Baby I'm Blue"	
2634	"See"/"Away Away"	
2654	"Carry Me Back"/"Real Thing"	
2695	"Hold On"/"I Believe"	

MOTOWN
•

Motown and Motown subsidiary label 45 RPM single releases represent a major innovation in early and mid-60's rhythm and blues. The decade of Motown began in 1959 with three releases: "Come To Me" by Marv Johnson; "Merry-Go-Round" by Eddie Holland; and the hard-hitting "Money" by Barrett Strong, obtained by Motown from the Anna label. Other early Motown releases were the basic rhythm and blues of "Bye Bye Baby" by Mary Wells on Motown; The Miracles' "Shop Around" and The Marvelettes' "Please Mr. Postman" on Tamla; and pounding-beat singles by Martha and The Vandellas on Gordy and by The Contours on Motown and Gordy. During this early period, The Supremes recorded several rhythmic Tamla and Motown label singles, while The Temptations issued two Miracle label releases, each with spotty success. Several other of Motown's most successful performers were drawn from small Detroit labels: Junior Walker from the Harvey label; The Spinners from Tri-Phi; and Edwin Starr and The Fantastic Four from the Ric-Tic label.

The period of solidly rhythmic Motown releases continued until early 1965, when two super soul groups emerged: The Supremes with "Where Did Our Love Go" and The Temptations with "My Girl." The popularity of The Supremes and The Temptations profoundly influenced not only the sound and style of Motown, it eventually transformed the whole spectrum of rhythm and blues into "soul music"—a refined, sophisticated sound that is less primitive in execution than rhythm and blues. The evolving soul music form was best represented in this early transitional stage by The Supremes and The Temptations along with a select range of other Motown label performers.

The soul style prevailed from 1965 through 1969. During this period the Motown complex dominated soul music, and a few selected performers almost exclusively occupied the Motown roster of 45 RPM releases. This ready-made hit approach was at its zenith during the years 1967 through 1969, when all Tamla label releases (Tamla 54156 through 54190) were recorded by five proven names—Smokey Robinson and The Miracles, Marvin Gaye, The Marvelettes, Stevie Wonder and The Isley Brothers. Not coincidentally, almost all of these records were hits. Obviously, this very hit-oriented formula left little room for the exposure of unproven soul music artists or for innovative styles to break through. This is not to say that Motown didn't create excellent soul music—in point of fact, a great percentage of these recordings were superb. Nevertheless, as Motown came to dominate soul music, its highly commercial approach to single releases inevitably inhibited soul.

Scarcity and Value

Several early Motown label releases are now fairly rare and have aroused corresponding collector interest. Motown #1, "Bad Girl" by The Miracles, was a reissue of the Chess label original. Being a very limited promotional release, today it is quite rare and valued in the $20 range. "Shake Sherry" by The Contours was a Motown label original that became a hit on Gordy. It is now extremely scarce on Motown—perhaps even rarer than Motown #1. The special Christmas 45 RPM issue by The Miracles (Motown EX 009), was pressed only on a disc jockey promotional label with an extremely small number of pressings—again it's extremely rare and worth between $15 and $20. Marv Johnson's "Come To Me" (Tamla 101) was a very limited pressing and is worth over $10. The two Tamla label issues by The Supremes are fairly scarce, bringing from $5 to $10. Also in the $5 plus range are The Contours' two releases on Motown (Motown 1008 and 1012) and Gladys Knight and The Pips' "Ching Chong" on Brunswick. Releases by The Spinners on Tri Phi and by The Temptations on Miracle can bring over $2.

As far as can be determined, the Tammi Terrell single (Motown 1115) was the only Motown or Tamla label release that was given an issue number and remained unissued. Any advance disc jockey copies that were made available would be very valuable.

Also, several short-lived Motown subsidiary labels, each issuing only a few 45's are now in demand. These labels include Mel-O-Dy, Rip-Cor and Pirate.

Collectors of Motown label singles often concentrate on "running" the entire series. Much of the better known material is relatively easy to locate. Early singles by obscure Motown-Tamla artists are more difficult to acquire. For instance, The Satintones had four Motown issues (Motown 1000, 1006, 1010 and 1020), and The Valadiers had two releases on Gordy (Gordy 7003 and 7013). Since none of these were hits, none were available for long and all of these are currently scarce.

Barrett Strong

Barrett Strong had a solitary best-seller, the Anna label original "Money." "Money" is of special interest and significance. With the exception of two short-lived, limited issues—Tamla 101 by Marv Johnson and Tamla 102 by Eddie Holland—it was the initial Motown-Tamla single and the only issue with a 50's release date. "Money" was great, hard-driving rock and roll, typical of a late 50's Detroit rhythm and blues sound.

Single Releases

Anna
1111	"Money"/"Oh I Apologize"	1959
	(also on Tamla 54027)	
1116	"You Knows What To Do"/"Yes No Maybe	
	So" (also on Tamla 54029)	

Tamla
54033	"Whirlwind"/"I'm Gonna Cry"	1960
54035	"Money And Me"/"You Got What It Takes"	1961
54043	"Misery"/"Two Wrongs Don't Make A Right"	

Mary Wells

Mary Wells' "Bye Bye Baby" was the first stone smash hit released on the parent Motown label. "Bye Bye Baby" is a jolting, solidly rhythmic recording with an aggressive instrumental and vocal delivery. "The One Who Really Loves You" was Mary Wells' next major hit. It contained some of the likable beat and feel of "Bye Bye Baby," as did her next three singles.

"My Guy" and "Once Upon A Time," a duet with Marvin Gaye, were Mary Wells' biggest sellers. They represented a more softly produced yet still potent Mary Wells vocal delivery. The single releases on later labels were generally not of hit caliber, but "Dear Lover" on Atco was a fine effort and sold well.

Mary Wells was unique to Motown. Her voice and material could never be adapted to a strict pop-soul mold, but she was able to use the very pleasant Motown approach to hit advantage with her energetic up-tempo style.

Single Releases

Motown
1003	"Bye Bye Baby"/"Please Forgive Me"	1960

1011 "I Don't Want To Take A Chance"/"I'm So   1961
    Sorry"
1016 "Strange Love"/"Come To Me"
1024 "The One Who Really Loves You"/"I'm   1962
    Gonna Stay"
1032 "You Beat Me To The Punch"/"Old Love"
1035 "Two Lovers"/"Operator"
1039 "Laughing Boy"/"Two Wrongs Don't Make   1963
    A Right"
1042 "Your Old Stand By"/"What Love Has
    Joined Together"
1048 "What's Easy For Two Is So Hard For One"/   1964
    "You Lost The Sweetest Boy"
1056 "My Guy"/"Oh Little Boy"
1057 "Once Upon A Time"/"What's The Matter
    With You Baby" (with Marvin Gaye)

20th Century Fox

544 "Ain't It The Truth"/"Stop Taking Me For   1964
    Granted"
555 "Use Your Head"/"Everlovin' Boy"   1965
570 "Why Don't You Let Yourself Go"/"Never
    Never Leave Me"
590 "He's A Lover"/"I'm Learnin' "
606 "Me Without You"/"I'm Sorry"

Atco

6392 "Dear Lover"/"Can't You See"   1965
6423 "Such A Sweet Thing"/"Keep Me In   1966
    Suspense"
6436 "Fancy Free"/"Me And My Baby"
6469 "Set My Soul On Fire"/"Coming Home"   1967

Jubilee

5621 "The Doctor"/"Two Lover's History"   1968
5629 "Woman In Love"/"Can't Get Away From
    Your Love"
5676 "Never Give A Man The World"   1969
5684 "Dig The Way I Feel"

Marvin Gaye

Marvin Gaye's first major hit was the blues-flavored "Stubborn Kind Of Fellow," with vocal support by The Vandellas. Also good-sellers were the likable dance vocal "Hitch Hike" and "Pride And Joy." Gaye maintained success with such strong upbeat blues and gospel-tinged material as "Can I Get A Witness," "How Sweet It Is" and "Ain't That Peculiar."

In 1967 Marvin Gaye began a happy recording alliance with the late Tammi Terrell. An instantly successful combination, the duo hit well with the smooth "Ain't No Mountain High Enough" and hit enormously well with their perfect rendition of the romantic soul ballad, the irresistible "Your Precious Love."

Marvin Gaye neatly blended his engaging vocal delivery with excellent upbeat soul material in the crisp performance of "I Heard It Through The Grapevine" (an earlier Gladys Knight and The Pips hit) and "Too Busy Thinking About My Baby," his biggest 60's hits.

Single Releases

Tamla

54041	"Let Your Conscience Be Your Guide"/ "Never Let You Go"	1961
54055	"I'm Yours, You're Mine"/"Sandman"	1962
54063	"Soldier's Plea"/"Taking My Time"	
54068	"Stubborn Kind Of Fellow"/"It Hurt Me Too"	
54075	'Hitch Hike"/"Hello There Angel"	
54079	"Pride And Joy"/"One Of These Days"	1963
54087	"Can I Get A Witness"/"I'm Crazy Bout My Baby"	
54093	"You're A Wonderful One"/"When I'm Alone I Cry"	1964
54095	"Try It Baby"/"If My Heart Could Sing"	
54101	"Baby, Don't You Do It"/"Walk On The Wild Side"	
54104	"I Want You"/"What Good Am I Without You" (with Kim Weston)	

54107 "How Sweet It Is"/"Forever"

54112 "I'll Be Doggone"/"You've Been A Long 1965
Time Coming"

54117 "Pretty Little Baby"/"Now That You've Won
Me"

54122 "Ain't That Peculiar"/"She's Got To Be Real"

54129 "One More Heartache"/"When I Had Your
Love" 1966

54138 "Little Darling"/"Hey Diddle Diddle"

54141 "It Takes Two"/"It's Got To Be A Miracle"
(with Kim Weston)

54149 "Ain't No Mountain High Enough"/"Give A 1967
Little Love" (with Tammi Terrell)

54153 "Your Unchanging Love"/"I'll Take Care Of
You"

54156 "Your Precious Love"/"Hold Me Oh My
Darling" (with Tammi Terrell)

54160 "You"/"Change What You Can"

54161 "If I Could Build My Whole World Around
You"/"If This World Were Mine" (with
Tammi Terrell)

54163 "Ain't Nothing Like The Real Thing"/"Little 1968
Ole Boy, Little Ole Girl" (with Tammi
Terrell)

54169 "You're All I Need To Get By"/"Two Can
Have A Party" (with Tammi Terrell)

54170 "Chained"/"At Last"

54173 "Keep On Lovin' Me Honey"/"You Ain't
Livin' Till You're Lovin' (with Tammi
Terrell)

54176 "I Heard It Through The Grapevine"/"You're
What's Happening"

54179 "Good Lovin' Ain't Easy To Come By"/ 1969
"Satisfied Feeling" (with Tammi Terrell)

54181 "Too Busy Thinking About My Baby"/
"Wherever I Lay My Hat"
Keep It" (with Tammi Terrell)

54185 "That's The Way Love Is"/"Gonna Keep On

54187 "What You Gave Me"/"How You Gonna
Tryin' Till I Win Your Love"

54190   "Gonna Give Her All The Love I've Got"/
             "How Can I Forget"

Motown
1128   "His Eye Is On The Sparrow"/"Just A   1968
             Closer Walk With Thee" (by Gladys Knight
             And The Pips)

Stevie Wonder

Originally billed as Little Stevie Wonder, this teenage virtuoso recorded several infectiously exciting early 60's singles, including "Fingertips," a major hit reminiscent of Ray Charles' "What'd I Say" (Atlantic 2031). Wonder's delivery in his first six singles was consistently and effectively up-tempo. This rhythmic style was brilliantly displayed in his next major hit, "Uptight." Stevie Wonder experimented with the rolling-tempo pop ballad with "Blowin' In The Wind" and "A Place In The Sun." This conservative approach to rhythm and blues was consistent with the mid-60's Motown "pop-soul" sound, and though these songs were moderate hits, they were less effective than his later, earthier hits, the joyous "I Was Made To Love Her" and "Shoo-Be-Doo-Be-Doo-Da-Day." Stevie Wonder then returned to ballads with a bit more success with "For Once In My Life" and "My Cherie Amour." However, Stevie Wonder is at his best with positive upbeat material complementing his electrifyingly dynamic musical talents. Relying more on self-composed work in the early 70's, Stevie Wonder has become a major rock and soul music figure.

Single Releases

As by Little Stevie Wonder:

Tamla
54061   "I Call It Pretty Music But The Old   1962
             People Call It The Blues Pt. 1 & 2"

54070	"La La La La La"/"Little Water Boy"	
54074	"Contract On Love"/"Sunset"	
54080	"Fingertips Pt. 1 & 2"	1963
54086	"Workout Stevie Workout"/"Monkey Talk"	
54090	"Castles In The Sand"/"To Thank You"	1964
54096	"Hey Harmonica Man"/"This Little Girl"	
54103	"Sad Boy"/"Happy Street"	
54114	"Kiss Me Baby"/"Tears In Vain"	1965

As by Stevie Wonder:

Tamla

54119	"High Heel Sneakers"/"Music Talk"	1965
54124	"Uptight"/"Purple Rain Drops"	
54130	"Nothing's Too Good For My Baby"/"With A Child's Heart"	1966
54136	"Blowin' In The Wind"/"Ain't That Asking For Trouble"	
54139	"A Place In The Sun"/"Sylvia"	
54142	"Some Day At Christmas"/"The Miracles Of Christmas"	
54147	"Hey Love"/"Travlin' Man"	1967
54151	"I Was Made To Love Her"/"Hold Me"	
54157	"I'm Wondering"/"Every Time I See You I Go Wild"	
54165	"Shoo-Be-Doo-Be-Doo-Da-Day"/"Why Don't You Leave Me To Love"	1968
54168	"You Met Your Match"/"My Girl"	
54174	"For Once In My Life"/"Angie Girl"	
54180	"My Cherie Amour"/"Don't You Know Why I Love You"	1969
54188	"Yester-Me, Yester-You, Yesterday"/"I'd Be A Fool Right Now"	
54191	"Never Had A Dream Come True"/"Somebody Knows, Somebody Cares"	

As by Eivets Rednow:

Gordy

| 7076 | "Alfie"/"More Than A Dream" | 1968 |

Junior Walker and The All Stars

Junior Walker and his band, The All Stars, were the premier Motown instrumental unit. This rhythm and blues combo emphasized the saxophone in the major hit, "Shotgun," a rousing dance-beat recording. Follow-up issues "Do The Boomerang" and "(I'm A) Road Runner" featured this strong exciting tempo with Walker's vocals, while "Cleo's Back" and "Cleo's Mood" (originally issued on the Harvey label) were downbeat blues instrumentals. In 1968, Walker had his best-seller, "What Does It Take (To Win Your Love)," a restrained vocal with excellent background work by The All Stars.

Single Releases

Harvey

113	"Twist Lackawanna"/"Willie's Blues"	1962
117	"Cleo's Mood"/"Brainwasher"	
119	"Good Rockin' "/"Brainwasher Pt. 2"	

Soul

35003	"Monkey Jump"/"Satan's Blues"	1964
35008	"Shotgun"/"Hot Cha"	1965
35012	"Do The Boomerang"/"Tune Up"	
35013	"Cleo's Back"/"Shake And Fingerpop"	
35015	"(I'm A) Road Runner"/"Shoot Your Shot"	
35017	"Cleo's Mood"/"Baby You Know You Ain't Right"	1966
35024	"How Sweet It Is"/"Nothing But Soul"	
35026	"Money Pt. 1 & 2"	
35030	"Pucker Up Buttercup"/"Anyway You Wanta"	1967
35036	"Shoot Your Shot"/"Ain't That The Truth"	
35041	"Come See About Me"/"Sweet Soul"	
35048	"Hip City Pt. 1 & 2"	1968
35055	"Home Cookin' "/"Mutiny"	
35062	"What Does It Take (To Win Your Love)"/"Brainwasher Pt. 1"	1969
35067	"These Eyes"/"I've Got To Find A Way To Win Maria Back"	

35070   "Gotta Hold On To This Feeling"/"Clinging
To The Thought That She's Coming Back"

NOTABLE MOTOWN SINGLE ARTISTS

Marv Johnson

Marv Johnson's most successful records were his early aggressive rock and roll efforts. "Come To Me," Marv Johnson's initial release was originally issued briefly on an early version of the Tamla label and almost simultaneously acquired by United Artists for release as a single on their label. Follow-up releases, especially the classic "You Got What It Takes," were best-sellers. Johnson rejoined Motown in the mid-60's with limited success.

Single Releases

Tamla
101	"Come To Me"/"Whisper" (also on United Artists 160)	1959

United Artists
175	"I'm Coming Home"/"River Of Tears"	1959
185	"You Got What It Takes"/"Don't Leave Me"	
208	"I Love The Way You Love"/"Let Me Love You"	1960
226	"Ain't Gonna Be That Way"/"All The Love I've Got"	
241	"Move Two Mountains"/"I Need You"	
273	"Baby Baby"/"Happy Days"	1961
294	"Merry-Go-Round"/"Tell Me That You Love Me"	
322	"I've Got A Notion"/"How Can We Tell Him"	
359	"Oh Mary"/"Show Me"	
423	"Magic Mirror"/"With All That's In Me"	
617	"Come On And Stop"/"Not Available"	1962

Gordy

7042	"Why Do You Want To Let Me Go"/"I'm Not A Plaything"	1965
7051	"I Miss You Baby"/"Just The Way You Are"	1966
7077	"I'll Pick A Rose For My Rose"/"You Got The Love I Love"	1968

Eddie Holland

Eddie Holland had success with his first Motown release, the bounce-tempo "Jamie." Holland's later recordings, such as the Jackie Wilson-influenced "If It's Love," were not successful. By 1964, Holland had left recording in favor of writing and production work that contributed much to the very successful Motown "soul sound."

Single Releases

United Artists

172	"Merry-Go-Round"/"It Moves Me" (also on Tamla 102)	1959
207	"Magic Mirror"	1960

Motown

1021	"Jamie"/"Take A Chance On Me"	1962
1026	"You Deserve What You Got"/"Last Night I Had A Vision"	
1030	"If Cleopatra Took A Chance"/"What About Me"	
1031	"If It's Love"/"It's Not Too Late"	
1036	"Darling I Hum Our Song"/"Just A Few More Days"	1963
1043	"Brenda"/"Baby Shake"	
1049	"I'm On The Outside Looking In"/"I Couldn't Cry If I Wanted To"	
1058	"Just Ain't Enough Love"/"Last Night I Had A Vision"	1964

1063 "Candy To Me"/"If You Don't Want My Love"

Jimmy Ruffin

Jimmy Ruffin was an exceptional soul ballad artist. Ruffin's best and most successful effort was the good-natured stroll-beat recording "What Becomes Of The Brokenhearted."

Single Releases

Miracle

1	"Don't Feel Sorry For Me"/"Heart"	1961

Soul

35002	"I Want Her Love"/"Since I've Lost You"	1964
35016	"As Long As There Is L-O-V-E Love"/"How Can I Say I'm Sorry"	1965
35022	"What Becomes Of The Brokenhearted"/ "Baby I've Got It"	1966
35027	"I've Passed This Way Before"/"Tomorrow's Tears"	
35032	"Gonna Give Her All The Love I've Got"/ "World So Wide, Nowhere To Hide"	1967
35035	"Don't You Miss Me A Little Bit Baby"	
35043	"Everybody Needs Love"/"I'll Say Forever My Love"	1968
35046	"Lonely Lonely Man Am I"/"Don't Let Him Take Your Love From Me"	
35060	"Farewell Is a Lonely Sound"/"If You Will Let Me Know I Can"	1969

David Ruffin

David Ruffin underwent a lengthy hiatus as a single artist during the years he was lead vocalist for The Temptations. This period, 1962 through 1969, was the group's golden age. Returning to solo recording, Ruffin had two 1969 smash hits, "My Whole World Ended" and "I've Lost Everything I Ever Loved."

Single Releases

Check Mate
    1010   "Knock You Out"/"Mr. Bus Driver—Hurry"   1962

Motown
    1140   "My Whole World Ended"/"I've Got To Find   1969
           Myself A Brand New Baby"
    1149   "I've Lost Everything I Ever Loved"/"We'll
           Have A Good Thing Going On"
    1158   "I Pray Everyday You Won't Regret Loving
           Me"/"I'm So Glad I Fell For You"

Kim Weston

Kim Weston proved an effective duet partner for Marvin Gaye prior to Gaye's teaming with Tammi Terrell. Weston's strong vocal style was evident in her two up-tempo hits, "Take Me In Your Arms" and "Helpless."

Single Releases

Tamla
    54076   "It Should Have Been Me"/"Love Me All   1963
           The Way"
    54085   "Just Loving You"/"Another Train Coming"
    54100   "Looking For The Right Guy"/"Feel Alright   1964
           Tonight"
    54106   "A Little More Love"/"Go Ahead And Laugh"
    54110   "I'm Still Lovin' You"/"Go Ahead And Laugh"   1965

Gordy
    7041   "A Thrill A Moment"/"I'll Never See My   1968
           Love Again"

7046 "Take Me In Your Arms"/"Don't Compare
      Me With Her"
7050 "Helpless"/"A Love Like Yours"

Shorty Long

Shorty Long's first Soul label release was the bluesy "Devil With The Blue Dress," a later hit for Mitch Ryder and The Detroit Wheels. Long's own best-selling hits were mostly in a novelty vein, "Function At The Junction," "Chantilly Lace"—taken from the 50's Big Bopper (D 1008) original—and the smash hit version of "Here Comes The Judge," a happily short-lived 60's craze.

Single Releases

Tri Phi
1006	"I'll Be There"/"Bad Willie"	1962
1015	"I'll Be There"/"Too Smart"	

Soul
35001	"Devil With The Blue Dress"/"Wind It Up"	1964
35005	"It's A Crying Shame"/"Out To Get You"	
35021	"Function At The Junction"/"Call On Me"	1966
35031	"Chantilly Lace"/"Your Love Is Amazing"	1967
35040	"Night Fo' Last"/"Night Fo' Last" (instr.)	1968
35044	"Here Comes The Judge"/"Sing What You Wanna"	
35054	"I Had A Dream"/"Ain't No Justice"	1969
35064	"A Whiter Shade Of Pale"/"When You Are Available"	

Edwin Starr

Edwin Starr began his career with two novelty rock and roll smash hits for Detroit's Ric-Tic label, the catchy "Agent Double-O-Soul" and "(S.O.S.) Stop Her On

Sight." Starr's Gordy label issues included the hit "Twenty-Five Miles," an engaging dance record.

Single Releases

103	"Agent Double-O-Soul"/"Agent Double-O-Soul" (instr.)	1965
107	"Back Street"/"Back Street" (instr.)	
109	"(S.O.S.) Stop Her On Sight"/"I Have Faith In You"	
114	"Headline News"/"Harlem"	1966
118	"It's My Turn Now"/"Girls Are Getting Prettier"	

Gordy

7066	"I Want My Baby Back"/"Gonna Keep On Trying"	1967
7071	"I Am The Man For You Baby"/"My Weakness Is You"	
7078	"Way Over There"/"If My Heart Could Tell The Story"	1968
7083	"Twenty-Five Miles"/"Love Is My Destination"	
7087	"I'm Still A Struggling Man"/"Pretty Little Angel"	1969
7090	"Oh How Happy"/"Ooh Baby Baby" (with Blinky)	

Tammi Terrell

Tammi Terrell, whose life was cut short in the early 70's, specialized in the sweet, lighthearted style, apparent in her two best-sellers, "I Can't Believe You Love Me" and "Come On And See Me." Her greatest success came as a duet partner for Marvin Gaye and resulted in an impressive string of hits.

Single Releases

Motown

1086	"I Can't Believe You Love Me"/"Hold Me Oh My Darling"	1965
1095	"Come On And See Me"/"Baby Don'tcha Worry"	1966
1115	"Oh What A Good Man He Is"/"There Are Things" (unissued)	1967
1138	"This Old Heart Of Mine"/"Just Too Much To Hope For"	1968

The Four Tops

The Four Tops recorded infrequently in the 50's and early 60's with negligible success. "Baby I Need Your Lovin'," a professionally rendered ballad, was their first Motown release, and it became a major 1964 hit.

The Four Tops were a most professional vocal group whose confident vocals resulted in an impressive string of rock-beat hits: "I Can't Help Myself" in 1965, the energetically paced "Reach Out I'll Be There" in 1966 and the mellow "Bernadette' 'in 1967. In 1968, The Four Tops switched to such non-rhythm and blues compositions as "Walk Away Renee" and "If I Were A Carpenter"—middle-of-the-road arrangements rendered with flawless ease.

The Four Tops ranked among the most successful Motown vocal groups. They represented a good-natured approach to soul music and epitomized the professional best of Motown.

Single Releases

Chess

1623	"Kiss Me Baby"/"Could It Be You"	1956

Riverside

4534	"Pennies From Heaven"/"Where Are You"	1963

Columbia
  43356 "Ain't That Love"   ca. 1964

Motown
  1062 "Baby I Need Your Loving"/"Call On Me"   1964
  1069 "Without The One You Love"/"Love Has
          Gone"
  1073 "Ask The Lonely"/"Where Did You Go"   1965
  1076 "I Can't Help Myself"/"Sad Souvenirs"
  1081 "It's The Same Old Song"/"Your Love Is
          Amazing"
  1084 "Something About You"/"Darling I Hum Our
          Song"
  1090 "Shake Me, Wake Me"/"Just As Long As You   1966
          Need Me"
  1096 "Loving You Is Sweeter Than Ever"/"I Like
          Everything About You"
  1098 "Reach Out, I'll Be There"/"Until You Love
          Someone"
  1102 "Standing In The Shadows Of Love"/"Since
          You've Been Gone"
  1104 "Bernadette"/"I Got A Feeling"   1967
  1110 "7-Rooms Of Gloom"/"I'll Turn To Stone"
  1113 "You Keep Running Away"/"If You Don't
          Want My Love"
  1119 "Walk Away Renee"/"Our Love Is   1968
          Wonderful"
  1124 "If I Were A Carpenter"/"Wonderful Baby"
  1127 "Yesterday's Dreams"/"For Once In My Life"
  1132 "I'm In A Different World"/"Remember
          When"
  1147 "Don't Bring Back Memories"/"What Is A   1969
          Man"
  1159 "Don't Let Him Take Your Love From Me"

Smokey Robinson and The Miracles

The Miracles originally recorded several mild-selling
End label releases in the late 50's. "Bad Girl" on the Chess
label of Chicago, a beautiful ballad emotionally rendered

by Smokey Robinson, was also the Miracles' initial hit
record.

In 1960, The Miracles signed with the fledgling Motown
label of Detroit, their second release on Tamla proved to
be a monster hit, the upbeat classic "Shop Around." Two
versions of "Shop Around" were released on Tamla 54028.
The original was a straightforward, tightly performed production; the second version lost some of the impact of the
first production. Why two different versions were released
on the Tamla label is not known; only the second version
remains available.

The Miracles recorded some great ballads including the
bluesy "You Really Got A Hold On Me" and three plain-
tively sung hits, "Ooo Baby Baby," "The Tracks Of My
Tears" and "My Girl Has Gone." The Miracles also
recorded faster dance hits: "Mickey's Monkey" and
"Going To A Go-Go"—the flip side "Choosey Beggar" was
a fine love song. No other vocal group had as many consistently fine love ballads during the 60's. Smokey Robinson and The Miracles seemingly recorded hit ballads in
cycles—"I Second The Emotion" and "Yester Love" being
more sophisticated than their earlier recordings.

Single Releases

As by The Miracles:

End

1016	"My Mama Done Told Me"/"Got A Job"	1958
1029	"Money"/"I Cry" (also on End 1084)	

Chess

1734	"Bad Girl"/"I Need Your Baby"	1959
	(also on Motown #1)	
1768	"All I Want"/"I Need A Change"	

Tamla

54028	"Way Over There"/"Depend On Me"	1960
54034	"Shop Around"/"Who's Lovin' You"	
54036	"Ain't It Baby"/"The Only One I Love"	1961
54044	"Mighty Good Lovin' "/"Broken Hearted"	

54048	"Everybody Gotta Pay Some Dues"/"I Can't Believe"	1962
54053	"What's So Good About Goodbye"/"I've Been Good To You"	
54059	"I'll Try Something New"/"You Never Miss A Good Thing"	
54069	"Way Over There"/"If Your Mother Only Knew"	
54073	"You've Really Got A Hold On Me"/"Happy Landing"	
54078	"A Love She Can Count On"/"I Can Take A Hint"	1963
54083	"Mickey's Monkey"/"Whatever Makes You Happy"	
54089	"I Gotta Dance To Keep From Crying"/"Such Is Love Such Is Life"	
EX009	"Christmas Everyday"/"The Christmas Song"	
54092	"The Man In You"/"Heartbreak Road"	1964
54098	"I Like It Like That"/"You're So Fine And Sweet"	
54102	"That's What Love Is Made Of"/"Would I Love You"	
54109	"Come On And Do The Jerk"/"Baby Don't You Go"	
54113	"Ooo Baby Baby"/"All That's Good"	1965
54118	"The Tracks Of My Tears"/"A Fork In The Road"	
54123	"My Girl Has Gone"/"Since You Won My Heart"	
54127	"Going To A Go-Go"/"Choosey Beggar"	1966
54134	"Whole Lot Of Shakin' In My Heart"/"Oh Be My Love"	
54140	"Come Round Here—I'm The One You Need"/"Save Me"	

As by Smokey Robinson and The Miracles:

Tamla

54145	"The Love I Saw In You Was Just A Mirage"/"Come Spy With Me"	1967

54152	"More Love"/"Swept For You Baby"	
54159	"I Second That Emotion"/"You Must Be Love"	
54162	"If You Can Want"/"When The Words From Your Heart Get Caught In Your Throat"	
54167	"Yester Love"/"Much Better Off"	1968
54172	"Special Occasion"/"Give Her Up"	
54178	"Baby Baby Don't Cry"/"Your Mother's Only Daughter"	
54183	"Doggone Right"/"Here I Go Again"	1969
54184	"Abraham Martin And John"/"Much Better Off"	
54189	"Point It Out"/"Darling Dear"	

Gladys Knight and The Pips

While recording as The Pips, the group had a major hit on the Vee Jay label (obtained from the Huntom label of Atlanta) with "Every Beat Of My Heart," an understated rendition of the classic Johnny Otis composition. The Fury label release of "Every Beat Of My Heart" was a slightly different version of the same material, but the Vee Jay issue was by far the best seller. In the next year, Gladys Knight and The Pips achieved mild success with the bounce-tempo "Operator" and "Letter Full Of Tears"—the latter sung in an effectively bluesy style. These Fury releases had a heavy instrumental and group vocal backing heard in many other early 60's rhythm and blues records.

After several label switches, Gladys Knight and The Pips arrived with Motown's Soul label and the ripping smash hit, "I Heard It Through The Grapevine"—a driving rock and roll performance. Such later releases as "The Nitty Gritty" and "Friendship Train" were also exciting hits that featured an aggressive vocal group support to Gladys Knight's sultry lead singing.

Single Releases

As by The Pips:

Brunswick
55048　"Ching Chong"/"Whistle My Love"　　　　1958

Huntom
2510　"Every Beat Of My Heart"/"Room In Your　　1961
　　　Heart" (also on Vee Jay 386)

As by Gladys Knight and The Pips:

Enjoy
2012　"Love Call"/"What Shall I Do"　　　　　　1961

Everlast
5025　"I Had A Dream Last Night"/"Happiness"　ca. 1961

Fury
1050　"Every Beat Of My Heart"/"Room In Your　1961
　　　Heart"
1052　"Guess Who"/"Stop Running Around"
1054　"Letter Full Of Tears"/"You Broke Your　　1962
　　　Promise"
1064　"Operator"/"I'll Trust In You"
1067　"Darling"/"Linda"
1073　"Come See About Me"/"I Want That Kind Of
　　　Love" (by Gladys Knight)

Vee Jay
545　"Queen Of Tears"/"A Love Like Mine"　　　1963

Maxx
326　"Giving Up"/"Maybe Maybe Baby"　　　　1964
329　"Lovers Always Forgive"/"Another Love"
331　"Either Way I Lose"/"Go Away Stay Away"　1965
334　"Who Knows"/"Stop And Think It Over"

Soul
35023　"Just Walk In My Shoes"/"Stepping Closer　1966
　　　To Your Heart"

35033	"Take Me In Your Arms And Love Me"/"Do You Love Me Just A Little Honey"	1967
35034	"Everybody Needs Love"/"Stepping Closer To Your Heart"	
35039	"I Heard It Through The Grapevine"/"It's Time To Go Now"	
35042	"The End Of Our Road"/"Don't Let Her Take Your Love From Me"	1968
35045	"It Should Have Been Me"/"You Don't Love Me No More"	
35047	"I Wish It Would Rain"/"It's Summer"	
35057	"Didn't You Know"/"Keep An Eye"	
35063	"The Nitty Gritty"/"Got Myself A Good Man"	
35068	"Friendship Train"/"Cloud Nine"	

Motown
| 1128 | "Just A Closer Walk With Thee"/"His Eye Is On The Sparrow" (by Marvin Gaye) | 1968 |

The Spinners

The Spinners were one of the early Motown label groups that didn't really catch fire following the Motor City hit formula. The Spinners had several moderate hits on Motown and V.I.P., but they only achieved major soul group status after switching to Atlantic in the early '70's. While with Detroit's Tri Phi label, The Spinners had a best seller with the sympathetic "That's What Girls Are Made For." Their Tri Phi issues were simply produced "do-wop" recordings. The Motown label records were neatly rendered soul productions, "I'll Always Love You" being the best seller. The V.I.P. issue, "In My Diary," was a faithful version of The Moonglows' 50's original (Chess 1589). Though The Spinners of the 60's shone with all the gloss and style of the more successful soul music groups, they never achieved headline status.

Single Releases

End

1045	"Bird Watchin' "/"Richard Pry Private Eye"	1959

Tri Phi

1001	"That's What Girls Are Made For"/"Heebie Jeebie's"	1961
1004	"Love, I Found You"/"Sudbuster"	
1007	"What Do She Use"/"Itchin' For My Baby But I Don't Know Where To Scratch"	1962
1013	"I've Been Hurt"/"I Got Your Water Boiling Baby"	
1018	"She Don't Love Me"/"Too Young, Too Much, Too Soon"	

Motown

1067	"Sweet Thing"/"How Can I"	1964
1078	"I'll Always Love You"/"Tomorrow May Never Come"	1965
1093	"Truly Yours"/"Where Is That Girl"	1966
1109	"For All We Know"/"I Cross My Heart"	1967
1136	"I Just Can't Help But Feel The Pain"/"Bad Bad Weather"	1968

V.I.P.

25050	"At Sundown"/"In My Diary"	1969
25054	"At Sundown"/"Message From A Blackman"	

The Marvelettes

Predating Martha and The Vandellas and The Supremes, The Marvelettes became the first successful female Motown vocal group with their solid smash hit, "Please Mr. Postman." The Marvelettes were noted for aggressive, positive delivery in such early rock and roll records as "Playboy," "Beechwood 4-5789" and the compelling "Danger, Heartbreak Dead Ahead." The Marvelettes adopted a medium-tempo ballad style with such later single issues as "Don't Mess With Bill" and "The Hunter Gets Captured By The Game"—both were major hits. The Marvelettes remained consistently exciting throughout the decade.

Single Releases

Tamla

54046	"Please Mr. Postman"/"So Long Baby"	1961
54054	"Twistin' Postman"/"I Want A Guy"	1962
54060	"Playboy"/"All The Love I've Got"	
54065	"Beechwood 4-5789"/"Someday Someway"	
54072	"Strange I Know"/"Too Strung Out To Be Strung Along"	
54077	"Locking Up My Heart"/"Forever"	1963
54082	"Tie A String Around My Finger"/"My Daddy Knows Best"	
54088	"As Long As I Know He's Mine"/"Little Girl Blue"	
54091	"He's A Good Guy"/"Goddess Of Love"	1964
54097	"You're My Remedy"/"A Little Bit Of Sympathy, A Little Bit Of Love"	
54105	"Too Many Fish In The Sea"/"A Need For Love"	
54116	"I'll Keep Holding On"/"No Time For Tears"	1965
54120	"Danger Heartbreak Dead Ahead"/"Your Cheating Ways"	
54126	"Don't Mess With Bill"/"Anything You Wanna Do"	1966
54131	"You're The One"/"Paper Boy"	
54143	"The Hunter Gets Captured By The Game"/"I Think I Can Change You"	
54150	"When You're Young And In Love"/"The Day You Take One You Have To Take The Other"	1967
54158	"My Baby Must Be A Magician"/"I Need Someone"	

54166	"Here I Am Baby"/"Keep Off, No Trespassing"	1968
54171	"Destination Anywhere"/"What's Easy For Two Is So Hard For One"	
54177	"I'm Gonna Hold On Long As I Can"/"Don't Make Hurting Me A Habit"	
54186	"That's How Heartaches Are Made"/"Rainy Morning"	1969

The Contours

The Contours became the earliest successful Gordy label group with their two hard-hitting smashes, "Do You Love Me" and "Shake Sherry." Though The Contours had a hit in 1966 with "Just A Little Misunderstanding," the popularity of this gutsy rhythm and blues group diminished with the emergence of the more-refined soul of Motown.

Single Releases

Motown

| 1008 | "Whole Lotta Woman"/"Come On And Be Mine" | 1961 |
| 1012 | "The Stretch"/"Funny" | |

Gordy

7005	"Do You Love Me"/"Move Mr. Man"	1962
7012	"Shake Sherry"/"You Better Get In Line"	
7016	"Don't Let Her Be Your Baby"/"It Must Be Love"	1963
7019	"You Get Ugly"/"Pa I Need A Car"	
7029	"Can You Do It"/"I'll Stand By You"	1964
7037	"The Day When She Needed Me"/"Can You Jerk Like Me"	
7044	"First I Look At The Purse"/"Searching For A Girl"	1965

7052 "Just A Little Misunderstanding"/   1966
      "Determination"
7059 "It's So Hard Being A Loser"/"Your Love   1967
      Grows More Precious Every Day"

The Supremes

By far the most successful of the three major female
Motown groups, The Supremes recorded over a half dozen
songs before coming up with the major hit, "Where Did
Our Love Go." The Supremes originally performed in the
more aggressive vocal style favored by the more successful
Marvelettes and Contours. "Your Heart Belongs To Me"
was sung in the deadpan bluesy style of Mary Wells, while
"Run Run Run" was rendered in an exciting Vandellas
inspired fast-moving approach.

With "Where Did Our Love Go," The Supremes proved
that a more slickly produced, middle-of-the-road style
could have enormous hit appeal. This record was the birth
point of "Soul Music." "Baby Love" and "Come See About
Me" also became major hits in this commercially refined
style.

This "pop-soul" innovation influenced the recorded
format of all other Motown label artists. It not only contributed greatly to the refinement and taming of Motown
rhythm and blues, but also caused a dilution of rhythm
and blues in general. The Supremes brought this highly
commercial, saccharine style to its peak with "Stop! In
The Name Of Love," "Love Is Here And Now You're
Gone," "The Happening" and the pretentious "I Hear A
Symphony." During this period The Supremes recorded
some excellent upbeat singles, including "Love Is Like An
Itchin' In My Heart" and "You Keep Me Hanging On."

Later recordings became pop showcases for Diana Ross,
an approach evident in the self-conscious "Love Child."
Diana Ross soon left the trio, and the re-formed Supremes
continued to record successfully into the 70's. The entire
series of Supremes singles constitutes some of the best and
most commercial soul records of the 60's.

Single Releases

As by The Supremes:

Tamla

54038	"I Want A Guy"/"Never Again"	1961
54045	"Who's Loving You"/"Buttered Popcorn"	

Motown

1027	"Your Heart Belongs To Me"/"Seventeen"	1962
1034	"Let Me Go The Right Way"/"Time Changes Things"	
1040	"You Bring Back Memories'"/"My Heart Can't Take It No More"	1963
1044	"A Breath Taking Guy"/"Rock And Roll Banjo Band"	
1051	"When The Lovelight Starts Shining Through His Eyes"/"Standing At The Crossroads Of Love"	
1054	"Run Run Run"/"I'm Giving You Your Freedom"	1964
1060	"Where Did Our Love Go"/"He Means The World To Me"	
1066	"Baby Love"/"Ask Any Girl"	
1068	"Come See About Me"/"Always In My Heart"	
1074	"Stop! In The Name Of Love"/"I'm In Love Again"	1965
1075	"Back In My Arms Again"/"Whisper You Love Me Boy"	
1080	"Nothing But Heartaches"/"He Holds His Own"	
1083	"I Hear A Symphony"/"Who Could Ever Doubt My Love"	
1085	"Children's Christmas Song"/"Twinkle Twinkle Little Me"	
1089	"My World Is Empty Without You"/"Everything Is Good About You"	1966
1094	"Love Is Like An Itching In My Heart"/"He's All I Got"	

1097 "You Can't Hurry Love"/"Put Yourself In My Place"
1101 "You Keep Me Hanging On"/"Remove This Doubt"
1103 "Love Is Here And Now You're Gone"/   1967
      "There's No Stopping Us Now"
1107 "The Happening"/"All I Know About You"

As by Diana Ross and The Supremes:

Motown
1111 "Reflections"/"Going Down For The Third Time"
1116 "In And Out Of Love"/"I Guess I'll Always Love You"
1122 "Forever Came Today"/"Time Changes   1968
      Things"
1126 "Some Things You Never Get Used To"/
      "You've Been So Wonderful To Me"
1135 "Love Child"/"Will This Be The Day"
1137 "I'm Gonna Make You Love Me"/"A Place In
      The Sun" (with The Temptations)
1139 "I'm Livin' In Shame"/"I'm So Glad I Got   1969
      Somebody"
1142 "I'll Try Something New"/"The Way You
      Do The Things You Do" (with The
      Temptations)
1146 "The Composer"/"The Beginning Of The
      End"
1148 "No Matter What Sign You Are"/"The Young
      Folks"
1153 "The Weight"/"For Better Or Worse"
      (with The Temptations)
1158 "Someday We'll Be Together"/"He's My
      Sunny Boy"

The Temptations

Along with The Supremes and The Miracles, The Temptations were one of the most prolific and most successful Motown label vocal groups. Proficient at various recording styles, The Temptations originally performed ballads, including the lovely "Dream Come True." Yet The Temptations' first major hit was the fast-paced "The Way You Do The Things You Do." Established as a hit group, The Temptations returned to the melodic ballad and had enormous success with the fine "My Girl" and "I Wish It Would Rain," two giant soul music classics of the 60's decade. Up-tempo hits included the energetic "Get Ready" and the sparkling "Beauty Is Only Skin Deep." With "Cloud Nine," The Temptations began to use psychedelic gimmicks, with mixed results. "Psychedelic Shack" and their 1970 release, "Ball Of Confusion" (Gordy 7099), represent an excess of technique that detracts from the great talent of The Temptations.

Single Releases

Miracle

5	"Oh Mother Of Mine"/"Romance Without Finance"	1961
12	"Check Yourself"/"Your Wonderful Love"	1962

Gordy

7001	"Dream Come True"/"Isn't She Pretty"	1962
7010	"Paradise"/"Slow Down Heart"	
7015	"I Want A Love I Can See"/"The Further You Look, The Less You See"	1963
7020	"May I Have This Dance"/"Farewell My Love"	
7028	"The Way You Do The Things You Do"/ "Just Let Me Know"	1964
7030	"Midnight Journey"/"Keep Me" (with Liz Lands)	
7032	"I'll Be In Trouble"/"The Girl's Alright With Me"	
7035	"Girl (Why You Wanna Make Me Blue)"/ "Baby Baby I Need You"	

7038 "My Girl"/"Nobody But My Baby"
7040 "It's Growing"/"What Love Has Joined   1965
      Together"
7043 "Since I Lost My Baby"/"You've Go to Earn
      It"
7047 "My Baby"/"Don't Look Back"
7049 "Get Ready"/"Fading Away"   1966
7054 "Ain't Too Proud To Beg"/"You'll Lose A
      Precious Love"
7055 "Beauty Is Only Skin Deep"/"You're Not An
      Ordinary Girl"
7057 "(I Know) I'm Losing You"/"I Couldn't Cry
      If I Wanted To"
7061 "All I Need"/"Sorry Is A Sorry Word"   1967
7063 "You're My Everything"/"I've Been Good To
      You"
7065 "It's You That I Need"/"Don't Send Me
      Away"
7068 "I Wish It Would Rain"/"I Truly Truly
      Believe"
7072 "I Could Never Love Another"/"Gonna Give   1968
      Her All The Love I've Got"
7074 "Please Return Your Love To Me"/"How Can
      I Forget"
7081 "Cloud Nine"/"Why Did She Have To Leave
      Me"
7082 "Rudolph The Red Nosed Reindeer"/"Silent
      Night"
7084 "Run Away Child Running Wild"/"I Need   1969
      Your Love"
7086 "Don't Let The Joneses Get You Down"/
      "Since I've Lost You"
7093 "I Can't Get Next To You"/"Running Away
      Ain't Gonna Help You"
7096 "Psychedelic Shack"/"That's The Way Love
      Is"

Martha and The Vandellas

Martha Reeves and The Vandellas had early success with the dynamic rockers "Heat Wave" and "Dancing In The Street." In fact, though the style of Martha and The Vandellas became a bit more polished with the likable "Jimmy Mack" and "Honey Chile," The Vandellas never entirely abandoned their powerful, rough-edged approach to soul music.

Single Releases

As by Martha and The Vandellas:

Gordy

7011	"I'll Have To Let Him Go"/"My Baby Won't Come Back"	1963
7014	"Come And Get These Memories"/"Jealous Lover"	
7022	"Heat Wave"/"A Love Like Yours"	
7025	"Quicksand"/"Darling I Hum Our Song"	
7027	"Live Wire"/"Old Love"	1964
7031	"In My Lonely Room"/"A Tear For The Girl"	
7033	"Dancing In The Street"/"There He Is"	
7036	"Wild One"/"Dancing Slow"	
7039	"Nowhere To Run"/"Motoring"	1965
7045	"You've Been In Love Too Long"/"Love (Makes Me Do Foolish Things)"	
7048	"My Baby Loves Me"/"Never Never Leave Your Baby's Side"	
7053	"What Am I Going To Do Without Your Love"/"Go Ahead And Laugh"	
7056	"I'm Ready For Love"/"He Doesn't Love Her Anymore"	
7058	"Jimmy Mack"/"Third Finger, Left Hand"	1967
7062	"Love Bug Leave My Heart Alone"/"One Way Out"	

As by Martha Reeves and The Vandellas:

Gordy
7067	"Honey Chile"/"Show Me The Way"	
7070	"I Promise To Wait My Love"/"Forget Me Not"	1968
7075	"I Can't Dance To That Music You're Playing"/"I Tried"	
7080	"Sweet Darlin' "/"Without You"	
7085	"We've Got Honey Love"/"I'm In Love"	1969
7094	"Taking My Love"/"Heartless"	

NOTABLE MOTOWN VOCAL GROUPS

The Elgins

The Elgins were among several second-level Motown label vocal groups who produced a handful of very successful hits. The Elgins (known as the 50's Sensations) had a 1962 hit record, the infectious dance-tempo "Let Me In." As The Elgins, the group recorded two solid V.I.P. hits, "Darling Baby," a mellow love song rendered in a classic 50's style, and the sensitively sung "Heaven Must Have Sent You."

Single Releases

As by The Sensations:

Atco
6056	"Yes Sir, That's My Baby"/"Sympathy"	1956
6067	"Please Mr. Disc Jockey"/"Ain't He Sweet"	
6075	"My Heart Cries For You"/"Cry Baby Cry"	
6083	"Little Wallflower"/"Such A Love"	
6090	"My Debut To Love"/"You Made Me Love You"	1957
6115	"Romance In The Dark"/"Kiddy Car Love"	1958

Argo

5391	"Music Music Music"/"A Part Of Me"	1961
5405	"Let Me In"/"Oh Yes I'll Be True"	1962
5412	"That's My Desire"/"Eyes"	
5420	"Party Across The Hall"	

Junior

986	"That's What You've Gotta Do"/"You Made A Fool Of Me" (also on Tollie 9009)	1962
1006	"Baby"	
1010	"I Can't Change"	

As by The Elgins:

V.I.P.

25029	"Darling Baby"/"Put Yourself In My Place"	1966
25037	"Heaven Must Have Sent You"/"Stay In My Lonely Arms"	
25043	"It's Been A Long Time"/"I Understand My Man"	1967

The Fantastic Four

The Fantastic Four recorded a series of titles for the Motown competitor, Ric-Tic of Detroit. The group had a moderate hit with the plush ballad, "The Whole World Is A Stage." In 1968, The Fantastic Four hit with the skillfully performed "I Love You Madly." This record only became a major hit after it was obtained by Motown from Ric-Tic for a Soul label release.

Single Releases

Ric-Tic

119	"Live Up To What She Thinks"/"Girl Have Pity"	1966

120	"You Gave Me Something"/"I Don't Wanna Live Without You" (also on Ric-Tic 128)	1967
122	"The Whole World Is A Stage"/"Ain't Love Wonderful"	
130	"As Long As I Live"/"To Share Your Love"	
134	"Goddess Of Love"/"As Long As The Feeling Is There"	
136	"Love Is A Many Splendored Thing"/ "Goddess Of Love"	1968
137	"No Love Like Your Love"/"Man In Love"	
139	"I've Got To Have You"/"Win Or Lose"	
144	"I Love You Madly"/"I Love You Madly" (instr.) (also on Soul 35052)	

Soul
35058	"I Feel Like I'm Falling In Love Again"/ "Pin Point It Down"	1969
35065	"Just Another Lonely Night"	

The Originals

The Originals were relative latecomers among 60's vocal groups, yet their sound was firmly rooted in a 50's rhythm and blues tradition. The Originals' two 1969 hits, "Baby I'm For Real" and "The Bells" featured a romantic group vocal effort, complete with a classic saxophone instrumental break.

Single Releases

Soul
35029	"Good Night Irene"/"Need Your Lovin'"	1966
35061	"Green Grow The Lilacs"/"You're The One"	1969
35066	"Baby I'm For Real"/"Moment Of Truth"	
35069	"The Bells"/"I'll Wait For You"	

Bobby Taylor and The Vancouvers

Bobby Taylor and The Vancouvers, a white vocal group with a black lead singer, had a first time hit with the compelling "Does Your Mama Know About Me"—the lyrics focus upon an interracial relationship. The group featured a sweet sound, that matched well with professional Motown arrangements.

Single Releases

Gordy

7069	"Does Your Mama Know About Me"/"Fading Away"	1968
7073	"I Am Your Man"/"If You Love Her"	
7079	"Malinda"/"It's Growing"	
7092	"My Girl Has Gone"/"It Should Have Been Me Loving Her"	1969

The Jackson Five

The Jackson Five, in the 60's tradition of The Supremes and The Temptations, became the Motown "supergroup" of the 70's. Following in the footsteps of Chicago's Five Stairsteps group, this teenage Jackson family vocal group's initial single release, "You've Changed," was not especially successful. However, their initial Motown single was the smash hit "I Want You Back," which was quickly followed by a string of number one hits well into the 70's.

Single Releases

Steeltown

681	"You've Changed"/"Big Boy"	1968

Motown

1157	"I Want You Back"/"Who's Loving You"	1969

CHI-TOWN

•

The Chi-town Sound added a cool, refined element to rhythm and blues. Ironically, during the late 40's and throughout the 50's Chicago was the base for many Mississippi Delta country blues singers, and their blues influence appears in the work of several important early 50's Chicago vocal groups—most notably The Spaniels and The Flamingos. From the same era of Chicago rhythm and blues came The Dells, a group which opted for a dry, harmonious performance in the 1955 smash hit, "Oh What A Nite." In the late 50's, the Impressions successfully adopted this reserved approach to a pleasant, fuller sound, and paved the way for later recordings by numerous outstanding Chicago vocal groups and single artists.

The Dells

In the mid-50's The Dells recorded two outstanding love ballads, the delicate "Dreams Of Contentment" and the cool hit "Oh What A Nite." The Dells blended this "cool" sound and approach into the more commercial "Chi-town Sound." Throughout the early 60's, The Dells couldn't produce a hit, but in 1968, they recorded "O-O, I Love You," a beautiful partly spoken ballad which was successful. "Stay In My Corner," a drawn-out gently soaring vocal containing traces of the 50's Dells, was a stone smash hit that propelled The Dells into second-time-around stardom.

Later Dells' material tended towards flowery, occasionally pretentious lyrics, exemplified by "Hallways Of My Mind," or towards overly produced singles, as in the 1969 remake of "Oh What A Night." These flaws of material and production detracted from The Dells who were at their best, a straightforward vocal group with a simple uncluttered style.

Single Releases

As by The El Rays:

Checker

794	"Darling I Know"/"Christine"	1953

As by The Dells:

Vee Jay

134	"Tell The World"/"Blues At Three" (by Count Morris)	1955
166	"Dreams Of Contentment"/"Zing Zing Zing"	
204	"Oh What A Nite"/"Jo Jo"	1956
230	"Movin' On"/"I Wanna Go Home"	
236	"Why Do You Have To Go"/"Dance, Dance, Dance"	
251	"A Distant Love"/"O Bop She Bop"	1957
258	"Pain In My Heart"/"Time Makes You Change"	
274	"What You Say Baby"/"The Springer"	
292	"Jeepers Creepers"/"I'm Calling"	1958
300	"Wedding Day"/"My Best Girl"	
324	"Dry Your Eyes"/"Baby Open Up Your Heart"	1959
338	"Oh What A Nite"/"I Wanna Go Home"	
376	"Hold On To What You've Got"/"Swingin' Teens"	1961

Argo
5414	"God Bless The Child"/"I'm Going Home"	1962
5428	"Eternally"/"Bossa Nova Blues"	
5442	"Hi Diddley Dee Dum Dum"/"If It Ain't One Thing It's Another"	1963
5456	"Good-bye Mary Ann"/"After You"	

Vee Jay
595	"Shy Guy"/"What Do We Prove"	1964
615	"Oh What A Good Nite"/"Wait Til Tomorrow"	
674	"Stay In My Corner"/"It's Not Unusual"	1965
712	"Hey Sugar Don't Get Serious"/"Poor Little Boy"	

Cadet
5538	"Thinkin' About You"/"The Change We Go Through"	1966
5551	"Run For Cover"/"Over Again"	
5563	"Inspiration"/"You Belong To Someone Else"	
5574	"O-O, I Love You"/"There Is"	1967
5590	"Show Me"/"There Is"	
5599	"Wear It On Our Face"/"Please Don't Change Me Now"	1968
5612	"Stay In My Corner"/"Love Is So Simple"	
5621	"Always Together"/"I Want My Momma"	
5631	"Does Anyone Know I'm Here"/"Make Sure"	
5636	"Hallways Of My Mind"/"I Can't Do Enough"	1969
5641	"Sing A Rainbow—Love Is Blue"/"Hallelujah Baby"	
5649	"Oh What A Night"/"Believe Me"	
5658	"When I'm In Your Arms"/"On The Dock Of The Bay"	

The Impressions

The Impressions were quite possibly the finest, most distinctive rhythm and blues vocal group of the 60's. Originally featuring a Jerry Butler lead, The Impressions first scored with the expressive ballad, "For Your Precious Love." After the departure of Butler, The Impressions—then a trio—were favored with the flawless, polished lead of Curtis Mayfield. On the ABC label, The Impressions immediately hit with the poignant, mid-tempo "Gypsy Woman" and the very likable "It's All Right"—the latter is an early example of the delicate, well-produced Chi-town sound.

The Impressions were an ideal vehicle for the brilliant lyrical talents of Curtis Mayfield, who created compositions about a full spectrum of experiences. "Amen," "People Get Ready" and "Meeting Over Yonder" were joyously spiritual in effect, while "Woman's Got Soul" and the bright "Can't Satisfy" were celebrations of the sensual. Human and civil rights were portrayed in the early "Keep On Pushing" and the later "We're A Winner" and "We're Rolling On." "Choice Of Colors" was a thoughtful portrait of racial contrasts, while "This Is My Country" was a non-flag-waving view of America during a volatile point in time.

Single Releases

As by The Impressions:

Bandera
2504   "Listen To Me"/"Shorty's Gotta Go"   1957

As by Jerry Butler and The Impressions:

Falcon
1013   "For Your Precious Love"/"Sweet Was The   1958
            Wine"
Abner
1017   "Come Back My Love"/"Love Me"

As by The Impressions:

Abner
   1023   "The Gift Of Love"/"At The County Fair"
           (also on Vee Jay 374)
   1025   "Señorita I Love You"/"Lonely One"   1959
   1034   "Say That You Love Me"

Vee Jay
   424   "Señorita I Love You"/"Say That You Love
           Me"   1962

ABC
  10241   "Gypsy Woman"/"As Long As You Love Me" 1961
  10289   "Can't You See"/"Grow Closer Together"   1962
  10328   "Little Young Lover"/"Never Let Me Go"
  10357   "You've Come Home"/"Minstrel And
           Queen"
  10386   "I'm The One Who Loves You"   1963
  10431   "Sad Sad Girl And Boy"/"Twist And Limbo"
  10487   "It's All Right"/"You'll Want Me Back"
  10511   "Talking About My Baby"/"Never Too Much
           Love"
  10544   "I'm So Proud"/"I Made A Mistake"   1964
  10554   "Keep On Pushing"/"I Love You"
  10581   "You Must Believe Me"/"See The Real Me"
  10602   "Amen"/"Long Long Winter"
  10622   "People Get Ready"/"I've Been Trying"   1965
  10647   "Woman's Got Soul"/"Get Up And Move"
  10670   "Meeting Over Yonder"/"I've Found That
           I've Lost"
  10710   "Never Could You Be"/"I Need You"
  10725   "Just One Kiss From You"/"Twilight Time"
  10750   "You've Been Cheating"/"Man Oh Man"
  10761   "Since I Lost The One I Love"/"Falling In   1966
           Love With You"
  10789   "Too Slow"/"No One Else"
  10831   "Can't Satisfy"/"This Must End"
  10900   "You Always Hurt Me"/"Little Girl"   1967

10932	"You've Got Me Running"/"It's Hard To Believe"	
10964	"I Can't Stay Away From You"/"You Ought To Be In Heaven"	
11022	"We're A Winner"/"It's All Over"	
11071	"We're Rolling On Pt. 1 & 2"	1968
11103	"I Loved And I Lost"/"Up Up And Away"	
11135	"Don't Cry My Love"/"Sometimes I Wonder"	
11188	"Just Before Sunrise"/"East Of Java"	

Curtom

1932	"Fool For You"/"I'm Loving Nothing"	1968
1934	"This Is My Country"/"My Woman's Love"	
1937	"My Deceiving Heart"/"You Want Somebody Else"	1969
1940	"Seven Years"/"The Girl I Find"	
1943	"Choice Of Colors"/"Mighty Mighty (Spade & Whitey)"	

Jerry Butler

A major exponent of "Chi-town," Jerry Butler's deeply rich voice—evident in the mellow rendition of "For Your Precious Love"—was perfectly suited for the love ballad, but as a single artist for Vee Jay Records, his first hits were the up-tempo "He Will Break Your Heart," "Find Another Girl" and "I'm A Telling You." Butler's first ballad hit was the silky rhythm and blues classic, "Make It Easy On Yourself." In late 1963, Butler recorded "Need To Belong," a fine ballad and one of the first single recordings in the highly sophisticated 60's Chi-town sound and style. "Need To Belong," "I've Been Trying" (later a major hit for The Impressions), and "I Stand Accused" influenced other Chicago artists, especially The Impressions, Gene Chandler and Billy Butler and The Chanters.

When Vee Jay folded in 1966, Jerry Butler signed with Mercury. After the label switch, Butler had a major string of hits that began with the haunting "Never Give You Up," and the emotionally sung medium-tempo ballads,

"Hey Western Union Man" and "Only The Strong Survive."

Jerry Butler was labeled "The Ice Man." His coolly sophisticated style was performed in a satisfying emotional way. His unique voice ideally lent itself to the Chi-town sound and style and contributed much to 60's rhythm and blues.

Single Releases

Abner
1024	"Lost"/"One By One"	1959
1028	"Hold Me My Darling"/"Rainbow Valley"	
1030	"I Was Wrong"/"Couldn't Go To Sleep"	
1035	"A Lonely Soldier"/"I Found A Love"	

Vee Jay
354	"He Will Break Your Heart"/"Thanks To You"	1960
371	"Silent Night"/"O Holy Night"	
375	"Find Another Girl"/"When Trouble Calls"	1961
390	"I'm A Telling You"/"I See A Fool"	
396	"For Your Precious Love"/"Sweet Was The Wine"	
405	"Moon River"/"Aware Of Love"	
426	"Isle Of Sirens"/"Chi Town"	
451	"Make It Easy On Yourself"/"It's Too Late"	1962
463	"You Can Run"/"I'm The One"	
475	"You Go Right Through Me"/"Theme From Tara Bulba The Wishing Star"	
486	"You Won't Be Sorry"/"Whatever You Want"	1963
526	"I Almost Lost My Mind"/"Strawberries"	
534	"Where's The Girl"/"How Beautifully You Lie"	
556	"A Woman With Soul"/"Just A Little Bit"	
567	"Need To Belong"/"Give Me Your Love"	
588	"I've Been Trying"/"Giving Up On Love"	1964
598	"I Stand Accused"/"I Don't Want To Hear Anymore"	

613 "Let It Be Me"/"Ain't That Loving You
       Baby" (with Betty Everett)
633 "Love Is Strange"/"Smile" (with Betty
       Everett)
651 "Good Times"/"I've Grown Accustomed To   1965
       Her Face"
676 "Since I Don't Have You"/"Just Be True"
       (with Betty Everett)
696 "I Can't Stand To See You Cry"/"Nobody
       Needs Your Love"
707 "Believe In Me"/"Just For You"
715 "Give It Up"/"For Your Precious Love"   1966

Mercury
72592 "Love"/"Loneliness"   1966
72625 "You Make Me Feel Like Someone"/"For
         What You Made Of Me"
72648 "I Dig You Baby"/"Some Kinda Magic"   1967
72721 "Mr. Dream Merchant"/"Cause I Love You
         So"
72764 "Lost"/"You Don't Know What You Got Until
         You Lose It"
72798 "Never Give You Up"/"Beside You"   1968
72850 "Hey Western Union Man"/"Just Can't
         Forget About You"
72876 "Are You Happy"/"I Still Love You"
72898 "Only The Strong Survive"/"Just Because I
         Really Love You"   1969
72929 "Moody Woman"/"Go Away—Find Yourself"
72960 "A Brand New Me"/"What's The Use Of
         Breaking Up"
72991 "Don't Let Love Hang You Up"/"Walking
         Around In Teardrops"

Billy Stewart

Nicknamed "motorboat mouth," the late Billy Stewart's
stuttering vocal style was effective in the fine "Reap What

You Sow." The understated, soberly expressed ballads "I Do Love You" and "Sitting In The Park" were both consistently selling 60's rhythm and blues hits. "Summertime," Stewart's major hit, was an aggressive, rapid-fire version of the standard.

Single Releases

Chess
1625	"Billy's Blues Pt. 1 & 2" (also on Argo 5256)	1956

Okeh
7095	"Billy's Heartache"/"Baby You Are My Only Love"	1957

Chess
1820	"Reap What You Sow"/"Fat Boy"	1962
1835	"True Fine Lovin' "/"Wedding Bells"	
1852	"Oh What Can The Matter Be"/"Scramble"	1963
1868	"Strange Feeling"/"Sugar And Spice"	
1888	"Count Me Out"/"A Fat Boy Can Cry"	1964
1905	"My Sweet Señorita"/"Tell It Like It 'Tis"	
1922	"I Do Love You"/"Keep Loving"	
1932	"Sitting In The Park"/"Once Again"	
1941	"How Nice It Is"/"No Girl"	1965
1948	"Mountain Of Love"/"Because I Love You"	
1960	"Love Me"/"Why Am I Lonely"	1966
1966	"Summertime"/"To Love To Love"	
1978	"Secret Love"/"Look Back And Smile"	1967
1991	"Everyday I Have The Blues"/"Ol Man River"	
2002	"Cross My Heart"/"Why"	
2053	"Tell Me The Truth"/"What Have I Done"	1968
2063	"I'm In Love, Oh Yes I Am"/"Crazy Bout You Baby"	1969
2080	"By The Time I Get To Phoenix"/"We'll Always Be Together"	

Betty Everett

Along with Mary Wells, Betty Everett was the second major female rhythm and blues artist of the early 60's. Everett's approach is that of aloofness, a sort of confident restraint. Her first hit was the peppery put-down "You're No Good." "The Shoop Shoop Song" and "Getting Mighty Crowded," rendered in the same detached, off-hand vocal delivery, were also successful. Betty Everett's very best seller was the 1969 Uni label single "There'll Come A Time," a ballad-paced recording with fine vocal shading.

Single Releases

Cobra
5019	"My Life Depends On You"/"My Love"	1957
5024	"Ain't Gonna Cry"/"Killer Diller"	1958
5031	"Tell Me Darling"/"I'll Weep No More" (also on Dottie 1126)	

C.J.
619	"Your Loving Arms"/"Happy I Long To Be"	1960

One-derful
4806	"Your Love Is Important To Me"/"I've Got A Claim On You"	1962
4823	"I'll Be There"/"Please Love Me"	1963

Vee Jay
513	"By My Side"/"Prince Of Players"	1963
566	"You're No Good"/"Chained To Your Love"	
585	"The Shoop Shoop Song"/"Hands Off"	1964
599	"I Can't Hear You"/"Can I Get To Know You"	
610	"It Hurts To Be In Love"/"Until You Were Gone"	
628	"Getting Mighty Crowded"/"Chained To A Memory"	
683	"The Real Thing"/"Gonna Be Ready"	1965

| 699 | "Too Hot To Hold"/"I Don't Hurt Anymore" | |
| 716 | "Trouble Over The Weekend"/"My Shoe Won't Fit" | 1966 |

ABC

10829	"In Your Arms"/"Nothing I Wouldn't Do"	1966
10861	"Your Love Is Important To Me"/"Bye Bye Baby"	
10978	"My Baby Loving My Best Friend"	1967

Uni

55100	"There'll Come A Time"/"Take Me"	1968
55122	"Better Tomorrow Than Today"/"I Can't Say No To You"	1969
55141	"Maybe"	
55174	"Been A Long Time"/"Just A Man's Way"	
55189	"Sugar"/"Just Another Winter"	

Joe Simon

Joe Simon's first hit record was the understated Vee Jay label release "Let's Do It Over." Joe Simon's relaxed approach and soothing voice were effective in his two must successful releases, the restrained "No Sad Songs" and "The Choking Kind."

Single Releases

Hush

103	"It's A Miracle'/"Land Of Love"	1960
104	"Everybody Needs Somebody"/"Call My Name"	
106	"Pledge Of Love"/"It's All Over"	
107	"Trouble"/"I Feel Your Face"	

GEE-BEE

| 077 | "My Adorable One"/"Say" (also on Vee Jay 609) | 1964 |

Vee Jay

663	"When I'm Gone"/"When You're Near"	1964
694	"Let's Do It Over"/"The Whoo Pee"	1965

Sound Stage 7

2564	"Long Hot Summer"/"Teenagers Dream"	1966
2569	"Too Many Teardrops"	
2577	"My Special Prayer"/"Travelin' Man"	1967
2583	"Just A Dream"/"Put Your Trust In Me"	
2589	"Nine Pound Steel"/"The Girl's Alright With Me"	
2602	"No Sad Songs"/"Come On And Get It"	1968
2608	"Hangin' On"/"Long Hot Summer"	
2617	"Message From Maria"/"I Worry About You"	
2622	"Looking Back"/"Standing In The Safety Zone"	1969
2628	"The Chokin' Kind"/"Come On And Get It"	
2634	"Don't Let Me Lose The Feeling"/"Baby Don't Be Looking In My Mind"	
2641	"San Francisco Is A Lonely Town"/"It's Hard To Get Along"	
2651	"Moon Walk Pt. 1 & 2"	

Gene Chandler

Gene Chandler originally lead singer for The Dukays, first hit with the stroll-beat "Duke Of Earl," a best-seller of 1962. In fact, "Duke Of Earl" was so successful that Chandler's next three Vee Jay label releases were attributed to "The Duke Of Earl." Returning to his Gene Chandler identity, he recorded the sleek ballad "Rainbow," a beautifully restrained example of early Chi-town. "Man's Temptation," the low-keyed "Just Be True" and "What Now" were all fine, unpretentious love songs. "Nothing Can Stop Me" was a medium-tempo hit that predated the "soul-pride" message recordings which became popular several years later. Gene Chandler's initial Checker label release was the engaging and very popular "I Fooled You This

Time." Chandler maintained a fine level of recorded performance throughout the 60's as a major exponent of the
marvelous Chi-town sound.

Single Releases

As by The Dukays:

Nat
4001	"The Girl's A Devil"/"The Big Lie"	1961
4002	"Nite Owl"/"Festival Of Love" (also on Vee Jay 430)	

Vee Jay
442	"I'm Gonna Love You So"/"Please Help"	1962
460	"I Feel Good All Over"/"I Never Knew"	
491	"Combination"/"Every Step"	1963

As by Gene Chandler:

Vee Jay
416	"Duke Of Earl"/"Kissin' In The Kitchen"	1962

As by The Duke Of Earl:

Vee Jay
440	"Walk On With The Duke"/"Lonesome Town"	1962
450	"Daddy's Home"/"The Big Lie"	
455	"You Left Me"/"I'll Follow You"	

As by Gene Chandler:

Vee Jay
461	"Tear For Tear"/"Miracle After Miracle"	1962
468	"Rainbow"/"You Threw A Lucky Punch"	1963
511	"Check Yourself"/"Forgive Me"	
536	"Man's Temptation"/"Baby That's Love"	

Constellation
112	"Think Nothing About It"	
114	"Soul Hootenanny Pt. 1 & 2"	1964
130	"Just Be True"/"A Song Called Soul"	
136	"Bless Our Love"/"London Town"	
141	"What Now"/"If You Can't Be True"	
146	"Everybody Let's Dance"/"You Can't Hurt Me No More"	1965
149	"Nothing Can Stop Me"/"The Big Lie"	
158	"Rainbow 65 Pt. 1 & 2"	
160	"Good Times"/"No One Can Love You"	
164	"Here Come The Tears"/"Soul Hootenanny Pt. 2"	
166	"Bet You Never Thought"/"Baby That's Love"	1966
167	"Fool For You"/"Baddy Ain't It A Shame"	
169	"I Can't Save It"/"I Can Take Care Of Myself"	
172	"Mr. Big Shot"/"I Hate To Be The One To Say"	

Checker
1155	"I Fooled You This Time"/"Such A Pretty Thing"	1966
1165	"To Be A Lover"/"After The Laughter"	1967
1190	"No Peace, No Satisfaction"/"I Won't Need You"	
1199	"River Of Tears"/"It's Time To Settle Down"	1968
1220	"Go Back Home"/"In My Body's House"	

Brunswick
55312	"Girl Don't Care"/"My Love"	1968
55339	"There Goes The Lover"/"Tell Me What Can I Do"	
55383	"There Was A Time"/"Those Were The Good Old Days"	
55387	"From The Teacher To The Preacher"/"Anywhere But Nowhere" (with Barbara Acklin)	
55394	"Pit Of Loneliness"/"Teacher Teacher"	

55405 "Little Green Apples"/"Will I Find Love" 1969
      (with Barbara Acklin)
55413 "Familiar Footsteps"/"Eleanor Rigby"
55425 "This Bitter Earth"/"Suicide"

NOTABLE CHI-TOWN VOCAL GROUPS

The Radiants

The Radiants performed aggressively sung ballads, including the mellow "It Ain't No Big Thing" and the cleverly worded "Voice Your Choice." Both songs were minor rhythm and blues hits. The 1967 release, "Feel Kind Of Bad" was an energetically rendered up-tempo song that became The Radiants' major hit.

Single Releases

Chess

1832 "Father Knows Best"/"One Day I'll Show 1962
      You"
1849 "Heartbreak Society" 1963
1872 "I'm In Love"/"Shy Guy"
1904 "Voice Your Choice"/"If I Only Had You" 1964
1925 "It Ain't No Big Thing"/"I Got A Girl" 1965
1939 "Whole Lot Of Woman"/"Tomorrow"
1954 "Baby You've Got It"/"I Want To Thank
      You Baby"
1986 "Feel Kind Of Bad"/"Anything You Do Is 1967
      Alright"
2021 "The Clown Is Clever"/"Don't Take Your
      Love"
2037 "Hold On"/"I'm Glad I'm The Loser" 1968
2066 "Choo Choo"/"Ida Mae Foster"

Billy Butler and The Chanters

Billy Butler and The Chanters recorded in a brisk, flashy style derived, in part, from The Impressions. Two of the group's biggest hits were "Nevertheless" and the high-speed "Right Track."

Single Releases

Okeh

7178	"Found True Love"	1966
7192	"I'm Just A Man"/"Gotta Get Away"	
7201	"Can't Live Without Her"/"My Heart Is Hurtin'"	1967
7207	"Nevertheless"/"My Sweet Woman"	
7221	"I Can't Work No Longer"/"Tomorrow Is Another Day"	
7227	"You're Gonna Be Sorry"/"You Ain't Ready"	
7245	"Right Track"/"Boston Monkey"	

Brunswick

55306	"Help Yourself"/"Sweet Darling"	1967
55347	"I'll Be You"/"Careless Heart"	1968
55372	"Thank You Baby"/"Burning Touch Of Love"	

The Five Stairsteps

The Five Stairsteps were an early teenage family vocal group who specialized in the emotionally rendered ballad with "You Waited Too Long" and "World Of Fantasy." The Curtom label releases, especially the fine "Stay Close To Me," were up-tempo workouts.

Single Releases

Windy C

601	"You Waited Too Long"/"Don't Waste Your Time"	1966

602	"World Of Fantasy"/"Playgirl's Love"	
603	"Come Back"/"You Don't Love Me"	
604	"Danger! She's A Stranger"/"Behind Curtains"	1967
605	"Ain't Gonna Rest"/"You Can't See"	
607	"Oooh Baby Baby"/"The Girl I Love"	
608	"The Touch Of You"/"Change Of Pace"	

Buddah

20	"Something's Missing"/"Tell Me Who"	1967
26	"A Million To One"/"You Make Me So Mad"	1968
35	"The Shadow Of Your Smile"/"Bad News"	

Curtom

1931	"Don't Change Your Love"/"New Dance Craze"	1968
1933	"Stay Close To Me"/"I Made A Mistake"	
1936	"Baby Make Me Feel So Good"/"Little Young Lover"	
1944	"Little Boy Blue"/"Madame Mary"	1969
1945	"We Must Be In Love"/"Little Young Lover"	

The Esquires

The Esquires had one smash hit, "Get On Up" an upbeat dance record with a distinctive high-voice lead. Their solitary Lamarr label issue, "Girls In The City," is a highly sophisticated gem and a truly beautiful recorded work.

Single Releases

Bunky

7750	"Get On Up"/"Listen To Me"	1967
7752	"Everybody's Laughing"/"And Get Away"	
7753	"You Say"/"State Fair"	1968
7755	"Why Can't I Stop"	
7756	"How Could It Be"/"I Know I Can"	

Wand

| 1193 | "You've Got The Power"/"No Doubt About It" | 1968 |
| 1195 | "I Don't Know"/"Part Angel" | 1969 |

Capitol

| 2650 | "Reach Out"/"Listen To Me" | 1969 |

Lamarr

| 1001 | "Girls In The City"/"Ain't Gonna Give It Up" | 1969 |

THE PHILLY SOUND

•

The "Philly Sound" is a generally Philadelphia-based approach to soul music. Essentially the sound is a refinement of the cool school of rhythm and blues which features dry, reserved vocal harmony. A late 60's innovation, the Philly Sound has since become a dominant 70's style—represented most successfully by The O'Jays and Billy Paul on the Philadelphia International label.

NOTABLE PHILLY SOUND ARTISTS

The Mad Lads

The Mad Lads' first recording was the ingeniously harmonic "Don't Have To Shop Around," released on the Volt label of Memphis. The next few recordings by The Mad Lads were medium-tempo ballads rendered in a droll vocal style.

Single Releases

Volt

127	"Don't Have To Shop Around"/"Tear-Maker"	1965
131	"I Want Someone"/"Nothing Can Break Through"	1966

The Intruders

The Intruders' "United"—lyrically romantic material rendered in a contrasting off-hand singing style—was a moderate 1966 hit. With the increasing popularity of the "Philly Sound," The Intruders had a major 1968 hit with their "Cowboys To Girls." This classic composition was a different version of the boy-meets-girl relationship theme by Gamble-Huff, the songwriting duo who largely created the distinctive Philly sound.

Single Releases

Excel
Gamble

209 "A Love That's Real"/"Baby I'm Lonely"
214 "Cowboys To Girls"/"Turn The Hands Of
  Time"   1968
217 "Love Is Like A Baseball Game"/"Friends No
  More"
221 "Slow Drag"/"So Glad I'm Yours"
223 "Give Her A Transplant"/"Girls Girls Girls"
225 "Me Tarzan You Jane"
231 "Lollipop"   1969
235 "Sad Girl"/"Let's Go Downtown"
240 "Every Day Is A Holiday"/"Old Love"

The Delfonics

The Delfonics' first major hit was the reserved mood-setting "La La Means I Love You," a classic example of the early ultracool Philly sound. The Delfonics had several other major hits with "Ready Or Not Here I Come" in 1968 and "Didn't I (Blow Your Mind This Time)" in late 1969–1970.

Single Releases

Cameo
472 "You've Been Untrue"/"I Was There"   1966
Fling
727 "There They Go"/"You Can Tell"   1967
Moon Shot
6703 "He Don't Really Love You"/"Without You"
Philly Groove
150 "La La Means I Love You"/"Can't Get Over   1968
  Losing You"
151 "I'm Sorry"/"You're Gone"
152 "Break Your Promise"/"Alfie"
154 "Ready Or Not Here I Come"/"Somebody
  Loves You"

156	"My New Love"/"Funny Feeling"	1969
157	"You Got Yours & I'll Get Mine"/"Loving Him"	
161	"Didn't I (Blow Your Mind This Time)"/ "Down Is Up Up Is Down"	

Archie Bell and The Drells

Archie Bell and The Drells produced the major 1968 hit, "Tighten Up," by blending quick-tempo guitar work and vocals into a transfixing dance beat. They then rendered "I Can't Stop Dancing" in a "Tighten Up" beat. The group also recorded love ballads, most notably the fine "Girl You're Too Young."

Single Releases

East West

| 55102 | "She's My Woman She's My Girl"/"The Yankee Dance" | 1966 |

Atlantic

2478	"Dog Eat Dog"/"Tighten Up"	1968
2478	"Tighten Up Pt. 1 & 2"	
2534	"I Can't Stop Dancing"/"You're Such A Beautiful Child"	
2559	"Do The Choo Choo"/"Love Will Rain On You"	
2583	"There's Gonna Be A Showdown"/"Go For What You Know"	
2612	"I Love My Baby"/"Just A Little Closer"	1969
2644	"Girl You're Too Young"/"Do The Hand Jive"	
2663	"My Balloon's Going Up"/"Giving Up Dancing"	
2693	"A World Without Music"/"Here I Go Again"	

Eddie Holman

Eddie Holman used his fine falsetto voice in capturing a fragile ballad style, evident in the early hit "This Can't Be True." "Hey There Lonely Girl," a record issued twice in 1969, was a sympathetic love song with classic 50's touches, one of the better soul records of the year.

Single Releases

Cameo

253	"Crossroads Pt. 1 & 2"	1963

Parkway

960	"This Can't Be True"/"A Free Country"	1965
981	"Don't Stop Now"/"Eddie's My Name"	1966
994	"Return To Me"/"Stay Mine For Heaven's Sake"	
106	"Am I A Loser"/"You Know That I Will"	
133	"Somewhere Waits A Lonely Girl"/"Stay Mine For Heaven's Sake"	1967
157	"Why Do Fools Fall In Love"/"Never Let Me Go"	

Bell

712	"I'm Not Gonna Give Up"/"I'll Cry 1000 Tears"	1968

ABC

11149	"I Love You"/"I Surrender'"	1969
11213	"Hey There Lonely Girl"/"It's All In The Game" (also on ABC 11240)	
11261	"Don't Stop Now"/"Since I Don't Have You"	
11276	"Cathy Called"/"I Need Somebody"	

SOUTHERN RHYTHM AND BLUES

•

Intense, shouting rhythm and blues, though somewhat overshadowed by mid-60's soul music, maintained a firm foothold throughout the decade. This gutsy sound was most successfully recorded by four very prolific singers: James Brown, Joe Tex and Ike and Tina Turner. In 1965, the release of Wilson Pickett's screaming "In The Midnight Hour" drew considerable attention to the funky "Memphis Sound" and electrified a somewhat dormant rhythm and blues scene. Aretha Franklin with her "I Never Loved A Man" and the follow-up "Respect" attracted across-the-board commercial success to this gospel-and-blues derived Southern sound and paved the way for an impressive roster of Memphis sound vocalists.

James Brown

James Brown was the most prolific rhythm and blues vocalist during the 60's. His basic approach was the intensely charged emotional vocal with solid instrumental backing. James Brown's first 60's recordings were for the most part pleading ballads—"I'll Go Crazy," "The Bells" and "Bewildered." "Think" and "This Old Heart" had a faster beat, but as with his 50's career, Brown's appeal was at first confined to the limited rhythm and blues market.

James Brown's first popular hit was the mostly instrumental "Night Train," a real dance mover. Brown continued to record similar dance-oriented singles, but didn't have another best-seller until the Smash label release, "Out Of Sight" in 1964. This classic, no-nonsense bullet propelled James Brown into super soul stardom. Because of contractual problems between Smash and King records, the later James Brown issues on Smash were strictly instrumental.

His return to King records resulted in a pair of excellent rock-and-roll paced singles, "Papa's Got A Brand New Bag" and "I Got You." James Brown returned to the drawn-out, wrenching vocal with "It's A Man's Man's Man's World," the aggressive "Cold Sweat" and "I Can't Stand Myself." These songs are all high-energy works. In 1968, James Brown recorded the irresistible soul anthem, "Say It Loud—I'm Black & I'm Proud," a major best-seller.

James Brown kept soul music of the 60's closely linked to Southern rhythm and blues roots with his influential power-packed writing, vocal and instrumental talents. But following his early most-distinctive releases, James Brown tended towards the monotonous with endless variations of "The Popcorn" and similar dances.

Single Releases

Federal

12258	"Please Please Please"/"Why Do You Do Me"	1956
12277	"Hold My Baby's Hand"/"No, No, No, No"	
12289	"Just Won't Do Right"/"Let's Make It"	
12290	"I Won't Plead No More"/"Chonnie On Chon"	
12292	"Gonna Try"/"Can't Be The Same"	1957
12295	"Messing With The Blues"/"Gonna Try"	
12300	"I Walked Alone"/"You're Mine, You're Mine"	
12311	"That Dood It"/"Baby Cries Over The Ocean"	
12316	"Begging, Begging"/"That's When I Lost My Heart"	1958
12337	"Try Me"/"Tell Me What I Did Wrong"	

12348	"I Want You So Bad"/"There Must Be A Reason"	1959
12352	"I've Got To Change"/"It Hurts To Tell You"	
12361	"Good Good Lovin' "/"Don't Let It Happen To Me"	
12364	"It Was You"/"Got To Cry"	1960
12369	"I'll Go Crazy"/"I Know It's True"	
12370	"Think"/"You've Got The Power"	
12378	"This Old Heart"/"Wonder When You're Coming Home"	

King

5423	"The Bells"/"And I Do What I Want"	1960
5438	"Hold It"/"The Scratch"	
5442	"Bewildered"/"If You Want Me"	1961
5466	"I Don't Mind"/"Love Don't Love Nobody"	
5485	"Sticky Suds Pt. 1 & 2"	
5524	"Baby You're Right"/"I'll Never Let You Go"	
5547	"I Love You Yes I Do"/"Just You And Me Darling"	
5573	"Lost Someone"/"Cross Firing"	
5614	"Night Train"/"Why Does Everything Happen To Me"	1962
5657	"Shout And Shimmy"/"Come Over Here"	
5672	"Mashed Potatoes U.S.A."/"You Don't Have To Go"	
5701	"Three Hearts In A Tangle"/"I've Got Money"	
5710	"Like A Baby"/"Every Beat Of My Heart"	1963
5739	"Prisoner Of Love"/"Choo-Choo"	
5767	"These Foolish Things"/"Feel It Pt. 1"	
5803	"Signed, Sealed And Delivered"/"Waiting In Vain"	
5829	"I've Got To Change"/"The Bells"	
5842	"Oh Baby Don't You Weep Pt. 1 & 2"	1964
5853	"Please Please Please"/"In The Wee Wee Hours"	
5876	"How Long Darling"/"Again"	
5899	"So Long"/"Dancin' Little Thing"	

5956   "Fine Old Foxy Self"/"Medley"

Smash
1898   "Caldonia"/"Evil"   1964
1908   "The Things I Used To Do"/"Out Of The
            Blue"
1919   "Out Of Sight"/"Maybe The Last Time"
1975   "Devil's Hideaway"/"Who's Afraid Of
            Virginia Woolf"
2008   "Try Me"/"Papa's Got A Brand New Bag"   1965
2028   "The New Breed Pt. 1 & 2"
2042   "Boo-Ga-Loo Pt. 1 & 2"   1966
2064   "Let's Go Get Stoned"/"Our Day Will Come"
2093   "Jimmy Mack"/"What Do You Like"   1967

Bethlehem
3089   "I Loves You Porgy"/"Yours And Mine"   1967

King
5968   "Just Won't Do Right"/"Have Mercy Baby"   1964
5999   "Papa's Got A Brand New Bag Pt. 1 & 2"   1965
6015   "I Got You"/"I Can't Help It"
6020   "Lost Someone"/"I'll Go Crazy"   1966
6025   "Ain't That A Groove Pt. 1 & 2"
6032   "Come Over Here"/"Tell Me What You're
            Gonna Do"
6035   "It's A Man's Man's Man's World"/"Is It Yes
            Or Is It You"
6048   "Money Won't Change You Pt. 1 & 2"
6056   "Don't Be A Drop-Out"/"Tell Me That You
            Love Me"
6064   "The Christmas Song Pt. 1 & 2"
6065   "Sweet Little Baby Boy Pt. 1 & 2"
6071   "Bring It Up"/"Nobody Knows"   1967
6072   "Let's Make This Christmas Mean Something
            This Year"
6086   "Kansas City"/"Stone Fox"
6091   "Think"/"Nobody Cares" (with Vicki
            Anderson)
6100   "Let Yourself Go"/"Good Rockin' Tonight"

6110	"Cold Sweat Pt. 1 & 2"	
6112	"America Is My Home Pt. 1 & 2"	
6122	"Get It Together Pt. 1 & 2"	
6133	"Funky Soul #1"/"Soul Of James Brown"	
6141	"I Guess I'll Have To Cry Cry Cry"/"Just Plain Funk"	
6144	"I Can't Stand Myself"/"There Was A Time"	
6151	"You've Got To Change Your Mind"/"I'll Lose My Mind" (with Bobby Byrd)	
6155	"I Got The Feelin' "/"If I Ruled The World"	1968
6159	"Maybe Good Maybe Bad Pt. 1 & 2"	
6164	"Shhhhhhhh"/"Here I Go"	
6166	"Licking Stick, Licking Stick Pt. 1 & 2"	
6187	"Say It Loud—I'm Black & I'm Proud Pt. 1 & 2"	
6198	"Goodbye My Love"/"Shades Of Brown"	
6203	"Santa Claus Goes Straight To The Ghetto"/"You Know It"	
6204	"Tit For Tat"/"Believers Shall Enjoy"	
6205	"Let's Unite The World At Christmas"/"In The Middle Pt. 1"	
6213	"Give It Up And Turn It Loose"/"I'll Lose My Mind"	1969
6222	"Soul Pride Pt. 1 & 2"	
6224	"I Don't Want Nobody To Give Me Nothing Pt. 1 & 2"	
6240	"Popcorn"/"The Chicken"	
6245	"Mother Popcorn Pt. 1 & 2"	
6250	"Lowdown Popcorn"/"Top Of The Stack"	
6255	"Let A Man Come In And Do The Popcorn Pt. 1 & 2"	
6258	"World Pt. 1 & 2"	
6280	"Ain't It Funky Now Pt. 1 & 2"	

Joe Tex

Joe Tex began his long recording career by issuing catchy novelty rhythm and blues songs for both King records and the Ace label of Jackson, Mississippi; none of these releases were sizable hits. In the early 60's, Tex recorded several James Brown-style pleading ballads for both the Checker label and the Anna label, again with very limited success.

In 1961, Joe Tex joined with the brand-new Dial label of Nashville. He waited until 1964 to release his first smash hit, the emotionally projected morality lesson, "Hold What You've Got." Joe Tex's next five singles were performed in this vein, the most successful entitled "I Want To."

Returning to novelty material, Joe Tex recorded the comic "SYSLJFM," "Show Me" and "Skinny Legs And All," each with a good-natured dance beat. This time these novelty records were resounding hits. Interspersed with these engaging releases were examples of Joe Tex's specialty, the message record—"I Believe I'm Gonna Make It" and "Don't Give Up." Happily, Joe Tex did not give up. He created a wealth of 60's rhythm and blues material.

Single Releases

King

4840	"Come In This House"/"Davy You Upset My Home"	1956
4884	"My Biggest Mistake"/"Right Back In Your Arms"	
4911	"I Had To Come Back To You"/"She's Mine"	
4980	"Pneumonia"/"Get Away Back"	
5064	"Ain't Nobody's Business"/"I Want To Have A Talk With You"	1957
5981	"Come In This House"/"I Want To Have A Talk With You"	1964

Ace

544	"Get It Out"/"Just For You And Me"	1957
550	"Little Baby Face Thing"/"Mother's Advice"	1958
559	"Charlie Brown Got Expelled"/"Blessed Are These Tears"	1959

572	"Don't Hold It Against Me"/"Yum Yum Yum"	
591	"Boys Will Be Boys"/"Granny Stole The Show"	1960
673	"Boys Will Be Boys"/"Baby You're Right"	

Anna

1119	"All I Could Do Was Cry Pt. 1 & 2"	1960
1124	"I'll Never Break Your Heart Pt. 1 & 2"	
1128	"Baby You're Right"/"Ain't It A Mess"	

Checker

1055	"You Keep Her"/"Don't Play"	1962
1087	"Sit Yourself Down"/"Get Close Together"	1963
1104	"Baby You're Right"/"All I Could Do Was Cry"	

Jalynne

105	"Goodbye My Love"/"Wicked Woman"	ca. 1963

Dial

3000	"The Only Girl"/"What Should I Do"	1961
3002	"One Giant Step"/"The Rib"	
3003	"Popeye Johnny"/"Hand Shakin' Love Makin' Girl"	1962
3007	"Meet Me In Church"/"Be Your Own Judge"	
3009	"I Let Her Get Away"/"The Peck"	
3013	"I Should Have Kissed Her More"/"Someone To Take Your Place"	1963
3016	"Blood's Thicker Than Water"/"I Wanna Be Free"	
3019	"Say Thank You"/"Looking For My Pig"	
3020	"I'd Rather Have You"/"Old Time Lover"	1964
3023	"I Had A Good Home But I Left Pt. 1 & 2"	
4001	"Hold What You've Got"/"Fresh Out Of Tears"	
4003	"You Got What It Takes"/"You Better Get It"	
4006	"A Woman Can Change A Man"/"Don't Let Your Left Hand Know"	

4011 "One Monkey Don't Stop No Show"/"Build   1965
Your Love"

4016 "I Want To"/"Funny Bone"

4022 "A Sweet Woman Like You"/"Close The
Door"

4026 "The Love You Save"/"If Sugar Was As   1966
Sweet As You"

4028 "SYSLJFM"/"I'm A Man"

4033 "I Believe I'm Gonna Make It"/"You Better
Believe It Baby"

4045 "I've Got To Do A Little Bit Better"/"What
In The World"

4051 "Papa Was Too"/"The Truest Woman In The
World"

4055 "Show Me"/"A Woman Sees A Hard Time"   1967

4059 "A Woman Like That, Yeah"/"I'm Going And
Get It"

4061 "C.C. Rider"/"A Woman's Hands"

4063 "Skinny Legs And All"/"Watch The One"

4068 "Don't Give Up"/"I'll Make Every Day
Christmas"

4069 "Men Are Gettin' Scarce"/"You're Gonna
Thank Me Woman"

4076 "I'll Never Do You Wrong"/"Wooden Spoon"   1968

4083 "Keep The One You Got"/"Go Home And Do
It"

4086 "Baby Be Good"/"You Need Me Baby"

4089 "That's Your Baby"/"Sweet Sweet Woman"

4090 "Buying A Book"/"Chicken Crazy"   1969

4093 "That's The Way"/"Anything You Wanna
Know"

4094 "We Can't Sit Down Now"/"It Ain't Sanitary"

4095 "I Can't See You No More"/"Sure Is Good"

4096 "You're Right Ray Charles"/"Everything
Happens On Time"

Ike and Tina Turner

Ike Turner has been recording and producing country blues artists, Howlin' Wolf and B.B. King among many others, since the very early 50's. Thus it is not surprising that his first recording with Tina Turner was the profoundly blues-soaked, energetic screaming vocal by Tina, "A Fool In Love." This song and their guitar-pounder "It's Gonna Work Out Fine" are early 60's rhythm and blues classics.

Throughout the period dominated by the pop-soul artist, Ike and Tina Turner recorded nothing but honest-to-god, gutsy rhythm rockers that paved the way (along with James Brown and Joe Tex) for the reemergence of the Southern blues influence in mid-60's rhythm and blues. Recording for a wide variety of labels, the Turners issued an extensive number of single releases, notably the intense "Tra La La La La" and "You Shoulda Treated Me Right" for Sue; the compelling "Please Please Please" for Kent; and the ripping smash hit, "Goodbye So Long" for the resurrected Modern label. It has been noted that many of these early titles reflect the ups and downs of the relationship between Ike and Tina, and this real life basis adds to these releases' impact.

Ike and Tina Turner adapted their blues-based style to the glossy Phil Spector sound with four remarkable Philles label releases. Though none were good-sellers, the Philles recordings are fine examples of the successful blending of blues with the best in rock production. In particular, "River Deep—Mountain High" stands out as a Spector classic.

Ike and Tina Turner pioneered the linking of rhythm and blues to hard rock in their 1969 release "I Want To Take You Higher"—originally done by the San Francisco rock group Sly and The Family Stone. This borrowing from rock music continued with the Turners' version of Creedence Clearwater's "Proud Mary," an absorbing, ever-building rolling rocker.

Single Releases

Sue

730	"A Fool In Love"/"The Way You Love Me"	1960
735	"I Idolize You"/"Letter From Tina"	
740	"I'm Jealous"/"You're My Baby"	1961
749	"It's Gonna Work Out Fine"/"Won't You Forgive Me"	
753	"Poor Fool"/"You Can't Blame Me"	
757	"Tra La La La La"/"Puppy Love"	1962
760	"Prancing"/"It's Gonna Work Out Fine"	
765	"You Shoulda Treated Me Right"/ "Sleepless"	
768	"Tina's Dilemma"	
772	"The Argument"/"Mind In A Whirl"	
774	"Please Don't Hurt Me"/"Worried & Hurtin' Inside"	1963
784	Don't Play Me Cheap"	
135	"Two Is A Couple"/"Tin Top House"	1965
138	"The New Breed Pt. 1 & 2"	
139	"Can't Chance A Break Up"/"Stagger Lee & Billy"	
146	"Dear John"/"I Made A Promise Up Above"	

Kent

402	"I Can't Believe What You Say"/"My Baby Now"	1964
409	"Please Please Please"/"Am I A Fool In Love"	
418	"Chicken Shack"/"He's The One"	1965
457	"I Wish My Dream Would Come True"/"Flee Flee Fla"	

Modern

| 1007 | "Goodbye So Long"/"Hurt Is All You Gave Me" | 1965 |
| 1012 | "Gonna Have Fun"/"I Don't Need" | |

Warner Bros.

5433	"A Fool For A Fool"/"No Tears To Cry"	1964
5481	"Finger Poppin' "/"It's All Over"	
5493	"Ooh Poop A Doo"/"Merry Christmas Baby"	

Loma

2011	"I'm Thru With Love"/"Tell Her I'm Not Home"	1965
2015	"Somebody Needs You"/"Just To Be With You"	

Sonja

2001	"If I Can't Be First"/"I'm Going Back Home"	1965
2005	"You Can't Miss Nothing That You Never Had"/"God Gave Me You"	
5000	"We Need An Understanding"/"Too Many Ties That Bind"	

Pompeii

66675	"It Sho Ain't Me"/"We Need An Understanding"	1966
66682	"You Got What You Wanted"/"Too Hot To Hold"	

TRC

963	"Beauty Is Just Skin Deep"/"Anything You Wasn't Born With"	1966
967	"Dust My Broom"/"I'm Hooked"	

Philles

131	"River Deep—Mountain High"/"I'll Keep You Happy" (also on A&M 1118)	1966
134	"A Man Is A Man Is A Man"/"Two To Tango"	
135	"I'll Never Need More Than This"/"The Cashbox Blues"	1967
136	"A Love Like Yours"/"Hold On Baby"	

Cenco

112	"Get It—Get It"/"You Weren't Ready"	1967

Innis

6666	"Betcha Can't Kiss Me"/"Don't Lie To Me"	1967
6667	"So Fine"/"So Blue Over You"	
6668	"Poor Sam"/"I Better Get Ta' Steppin' "	
3002	"You Can't Have Your Cake"/"The Drag"	1968

Blue Thumb
101	"I've Been Loving You Too Long"/ "Grumbling"	1969
102	"The Hunter"/"Crazy Bout You Baby"	
104	"Bold Soul Sister"/"I Know"	

Minit
32060	"I'm Gonna Do All I Can"/"You've Got Too Many Ties That Bind"	1969
32068	"With A Little Help From My Friends"/"I Wish It Would Rain"	
32077	"Treating Us Funky"/"I Wanna Jump"	

Liberty
56177	"I Want To Take You Higher"/"Contact High"	1969
56194	"Takin' Back My Name"/"Love Is A Game"	
56207	"Workin' Together"/"The Way You Love Me"	
56216	"Proud Mary"/"Funkier Than A Mosquita's Tweeter"	

The Ikettes

The Ikettes, Ike and Tina Turner's female backup vocal group, had several impressive hits as a separate recording act. "I'm Blue" is a throbbing-beat, pleading classic. Both "Camel Walk" and "Peaches N Cream" are great rock and roll dance-beat single releases.

Single Releases

Atco
6212	"I'm Blue"/"Find My Baby"	1961
6223	"Troubles On My Mind"/"Come On And Truck"	1962
6232	"Heavenly Love"/"Zizzy Zee Zum Zum"	
6243	"I Had A Dream The Other Night"/"I Do Love You"	

Teena
    1702   "Prisoner In Love"/"Those Words"   1963

Modern
    1003   "Camel Walk"/"Nobody Loves Me"   1964
    1005   "Peaches N Cream"/"The Biggest Players"   1965
    1011   "I'm So Thankful"/"Don't Feel Sorry For Me"
    1015   "Sally Go Round The Roses"/"Lonely For
           You"
    1024   "Da Doo Ron Ron"/"Not That I Recall"   1966

Phi-Dan
    5009   "What'cha Gonna Do"/"Down Down"   1966

Innis
    6667   "So Fine"/"So Blue Over You"   1967
    3000   "Here's Your Heart"   1968

THE MEMPHIS SOUND
•

As with Philles and Motown, the Stax and Volt labels represent a distinct rhythm and blues sound in the 60's. The forerunner of Stax (Satellite records) can be traced to 1960–1961, with that label's first hit, the bluesy instrumental "Last Night" by The Mar-Keys (Satellite 107). The first Volt issue was also an instrumental—"Raw Biscuits" by The Triumphs (Volt 100). Pioneer Stax-Volt recordings set an early instrumental course for the phenomenal blues-and-gospel derived "Memphis Sound." A broad Stax-Volt singles collection gives a complete overview of this major form of 60's soul music.

Aretha Franklin

A master of several separate vocal styles, Aretha Franklin first recorded two solid gospel singles for the Checker label of Chicago. Her first style transition was into jazz with renditions of such standards as "Try A Little Tenderness" and "Jim" along with Jolson's "Rock-A-Bye Your Baby With A Dixie Melody" and "Swanee." Several of her more effective Columbia label releases were with jazz-blues material, "Today I Sing The Blues" and "God Bless The Child" and with the upbeat "Won't Be Long"—a minor hit.

Aretha Franklin brought a powerful style to these Columbia jazz arrangements. Her provocative voice never lost the gospel edge apparent in her first Atlantic label release "I Never Loved A Man"—her first major hit on any label— and was suited to the emotionally charged, Southern-influenced Memphis sound which Atlantic records was strongly promoting. Aretha Franklin, often with the vocal backing of The Sweet Inspirations, recorded only hits for Atlantic during the later 60's.

Still another approach to style and material became evident with her 1968 version of "I Say A Little Prayer." This Bacharach song was originally recorded by pop-soul singer Dionne Warwicke, and though Aretha rendered it with a touch more feeling, it was basically performed in a pop vein. This changeover to such lighter material as the Lennon-McCartney composition "Eleanor Rigby" and "Gentle On My Mind"—popularized by Glenn Campbell—gave Aretha Franklin two major pop-soul hits.

Though an unusually versatile vocal artist, Aretha Franklin was undeniably most effective when given the opportunity to render blues-based material.

Single Releases

Checker

861	"Never Grow Old"/"You Grow Closer"	1957
941	"Precious Lord Pt. 1 & 2"	1959

Columbia

41793	"Today I Sing The Blues"/"Love Is The Only Thing" (also on Columbia 44951)	1960
41923	"Won't Be Long"/"Right Now"	1961
41985	"Maybe I'm A Fool"/"Are You Sure"	
42157	"Rock-A-Bye Your Baby With A Dixie Melody"/"Operation Heartbreak"	
42266	"Rough Lover"/"I Surrender Dear"	1962
42456	"Don't Cry Baby"/"Without The One You Love"	
42520	"Try A Little Tenderness"	

42625	"God Bless The Child"/"Trouble In Mind"	
42796	"Say It Isn't So"/"Here's Where I Came In"	1963
42874	"Skylark"/"You've Got Her"	
43009	"Soulville"/"Evil Gal Blues"	1964
	(also on Columbia 44441)	
43113	"Runnin' Out Of Fools"	
43177	"Winter Wonderland"/"The Christmas Song"	
43203	"Can't You Just See Me"/"Little Miss	1965
	Raggedy Ann"	
43241	"One Step Ahead"/"I Can't Wait Until I See	
	My Baby's Face"	
43333	"I'm Losing You"/"Sweet Bitter Love"	
43442	"There Is No Greater Love"/"You Made Me	
	Love You"	
43515	"Hands Off"/"Tighten Up Your Tie, Button	1966
	Up Your Jacket"	
43827	"Cry Like A Baby"/"Swanee"	
44181	"Lee Cross"/"Until You Were Gone"	1967
44270	"Take A Look"/"Follow Your Heart"	
44381	"Mockingbird"/"A Mother's Love"	1968
44851	"Jim"/"Friendly Persuasion"	1969

Atlantic

2386	"I Never Loved A Man"/"Do Right Woman	1967
	Do Right Man"	
2403	"Respect"/"Dr. Feelgood"	
2427	"Baby I Love You"/"Going Down Slow"	
2441	"A Natural Woman"/"Baby Baby Baby"	
2464	"Chain Of Fools"/"Prove It"	
2486	"Since You've Been Gone"/"Ain't No Way"	1968
2518	"Think"/"You Send Me"	
2546	"I Say A Little Prayer"/"The House That	
	Jack Built"	
2574	"See Saw"/"My Song"	
2603	"Tracks Of My Tears"/"The Weight"	1969
2619	"I Can't See Myself Leaving You"/"Gentle	
	On My Mind"	
2683	"Eleanor Rigby"/"It Ain't Fair"	

Wilson Pickett

A dominant force in the mid-60's Atlantic label group of
Memphis sound rhythm and blues artists, Wilson Pickett
began his recording career with the 50's rhythm and blues
vocal group, The Falcons. Pickett's high-powered scream-
ing style is evident in the fine 1959 hit record, "You're So
Fine" by the Falcons (Flick 001). Though "If You Need
Me" and "It's Too Late" are excellent rhythm and blues
ballads, Pickett enjoyed only fair success with his several
Double L label releases. In the long hot summer of 1965,
the dynamite record "In The Midnight Hour" catapulted
Wilson Pickett into major rhythm and blues stardom. The
"Wicked " Wilson Pickett had arrived. "In The Midnight
Hour" was the ideal showcase for Pickett's high-voltage
singing style and also served as the first major hit in the
soon to skyrocket Memphis sound. Pickett's follow-up
releases were consistent hits. These included the rock-beat
"Don't Fight It" and "Funky Broadway" and the emotionally rendered "I'm In Love," which recalled the excitement of his early Double L label releases.

Single Releases

Double L

713	"If You Need Me"/"Baby Call On Me"	1962
717	"It's Too Late"/"I'm Gonna Love You"	1963
724	"I'm Down To My Last Heartbreak"/"I Can't Stop"	

Verve

10378	"My Heart Belongs To You"/"Let Me Be Your Boy"	ca. 1963

Atlantic

2233	"I'm Gonna Cry"/"For Better Or Worse"	1964
2271	"Come Home Baby"/"Take A Little Love"	1965
2289	"In The Midnight Hour"/"I'm Not Tired"	
2306	"Don't Fight It"/"It's All Over"	

2320	"634-5789"/"That's A Man's Way"	1966
2334	"Ninety-Nine And A Half"/"Danger Zone"	
2348	"Land Of 1000 Dances"/"You're So Fine"	
2365	"Mustang Sally"/"Three Time Loser"	
2381	"Everybody Needs Somebody To Love"/	1967
	"Nothing You Can Do"	
2394	"I Found A Love Pt. 1 & 2"	
2412	"You Can't Stand Alone"/"Soul Dance #3"	
2430	"Funky Broadway"/"I'm Sorry About That"	
2448	"I'm In Love"/"Stag-O-Lee"	
2484	"I've Come A Long Way"/"Jealous Love"	1968
2504	"She's Lookin' Good"/"We've Got To Have Love"	
2528	"I'm A Midnight Mover"/"Deborah"	
2558	"I Found A True Love"/"For Better Or Worse"	
2575	"A Man And A Half"/"People Make The World"	
2591	"Hey Jude"/"Search Your Heart"	
2611	"Mini-Skirt Minnie"/"Back In Your Arms"	1969
2631	"Born To Be Wild"/"Toe Hold"	
2648	"Hey Joe"/"Night Owl"	
2682	"You Keep Me Hanging On"/"Now You See Me Now You Don't"	

Otis Redding

Otis Redding's earliest recordings are imbued with a primitive raw intensity. Redding's sole Bethlehem label recording, the twist-beat "Shout Bamalama" is a fine example of his style's development in the shouting tradition of Little Richard. Otis Redding remained a fairly obscure rhythm and blues artist for his first two years with the Memphis Volt label. He recorded several deeply felt ballads during these early years—"These Arms Of Mine," "Pain In My Heart" and "I've Been Loving You Too Long" along with one excellent fast blues recording, "Mr. Pitiful." Otis Redding's emergence with his first hit, the harshly rhythmic "Respect," coincided with the overnight success of the Memphis sound. The pounding upbeat approach with "Respect" ideally suited Redding's vocal abilities.

Unfortunately, it was Redding's well-publicized tragic death that partially led to his first major hit, "(Sittin' On) The Dock Of The Bay"—a sadly rendered piece. Volt-Atlantic records had a great deal of unreleased Otis Redding material that was subsequently issued on Atco label singles. Except for the fine "Hard To Handle," most of these records were merely adequate performances and sold only moderately. Otis Redding did not possess a great vocal talent, but he did provide several memorable rhythm and blues performances.

Single Releases

Bethlehem

3083	"Shout Bamalama"/"Fat Gal"	1960
	(also on King 6149)	

Finer Arts

2016	"She's All Right"/"Tuff Enuff"	ca. 1966
		(recorded earlier)

Volt

103	"These Arms Of Mine"/"Hey Hey Baby"	1962
109	"That's What My Heart Needs"/"Mary's Little Lamb"	1963
112	"Pain In My Heart"/"Something Is Worrying Me"	
116	"Don't Leave Me This Way"/"Come To Me"	1964
117	"Security"/"I Want To Thank You"	
121	"Your One And Only Love"/"Chained And Bound"	
124	"Mr. Pitiful"/"That's How Strong My Love Is"	1965

126 "I've Been Loving You Too Long"/"I'm
   Depending On You"
128 "Respect"/"Ole Man Trouble"
130 "I Can't Turn You Loose"/"Just One More
   Day"
132 "Satisfaction"/"Any Ole Way"   1966
136 "My Lover's Prayer"/"Don't Mess With
   Cupid"
138 "Fa-Fa-Fa-Fa-Fa"/"Good To Me"
141 "Try A Little Tenderness"/"I'm Sick Y'All"
146 "I Love You More Than Words Can Say"/   1967
   "Let Me Come On Home"
149 "Shake"/"You Don't Miss Your Water"
152 "Glory Of Love"/"I'm Coming Home"
157 "(Sittin' On) The Dock Of The Bay"/"Sweet 1968
   Lorene"
163 "The Happy Song"/"Open The Door"

Stax
216 "Tell It Like It Is"/"Tramp"   1967
   (with Carla Thomas)
228 "Knock On Wood"/"Let Me Be Good To You"
   (with Carla Thomas)
244 "Lovey Dovey"/"New Year's Resolution"   1968
   (with Carla Thomas)

Atco
6592 "Hard To Handle"/"Amen"   1968
6612 "I've Got Dreams To Remember"/"Nobody's
   Fault But Mine"
6631 "White Christmas"/"Merry Christmas Baby"
6636 "Direct Me"/"Papa's Got A Brand New Bag" 1969
6654 "A Lover's Question"/"You Made A Man
   Out Of Me"
6665 "When Something Is Wrong With My Baby"/
   "Ooh Carla Ooh Otis" (with Carla
   Thomas)
6677 "Can't Turn You Loose"/"Love Man"
6700 "Higher And Higher"/"Free Me"

Booker T & The MG's

Booker T & The MG's were the energetic instrumental combo who gave Stax records the early, quick-paced 1962 hit, "Green Onions." Booker T achieved his basic sound through the tight, funky organ and guitar combination that was the instrumental backbone for the powerful Memphis sound. Other fine single issues include "Chinese Checkers," "Can't Be Still" and the major rhythm and blues hits, "Boot-Leg" and "Hip-Hug-Her." These Booker T & The MG's instrumentals were uncommonly durable. One solid indicator that this sound was indeed classic 60's rhythm and blues is the fact that several of these records served as theme music for major rhythm and blues radio stations.

Single Releases

Stax

127	"Green Onions"/"Behave Yourself"	1962
131	"Jelly Bread"/"Aw' Mercy"	
134	"Big Train"/"Homegrown"	1963
137	"Chinese Checkers"/"Plum Nellie"	
142	"Fannie Mae"/"Mo Onions"	
142	"Tic-Tac-Toe"/"Mo Onions"	
153	"MG Party"/"Soul Dressing"	1964
161	"Can't Be Still"/"Terrible Thing"	
169	"Boot-Leg"/"Outrage"	1965
182	"Red Beans And Rice"/"Be My Lady"	
196	"Booker-Loo"/"My Sweet Potato"	1966
203	"Jingle Bells"/"Winter Wonderland"	
211	"Hip-Hug Her"/"Summertime"	1967
224	"Groovin' "/"Slim Jenkin's Place"	
0001	"Soul Limbo"/"Heads Or Tails"	1968
0013	"Hang Em High"/"Over Easy"	
0028	"Time Is Tight"/"Johnny I Love You"	
0037	"Soul Clap"/"Mrs. Robinson"	1969
0049	"Slum Baby"/"Meditation"	

Sam and Dave

Sam and Dave, "The Dynamite Duo," were a smashing 1966 success with the shouting blockbuster "Hold On I'm A Comin'." Their follow-up hit, "When Something Is Wrong With My Baby" is a slow vocal blues with gospel-shouting overtones. "Soul Man," Sam and Dave's biggest hit, was a perfect example of the duo's aggressive vocals. After the success of "Soul Man," Sam and Dave had no other best-sellers.

Single Releases

Roulette
4419	"I Need Love"/"Keep A Walkin' "	1964
4445	"No More Pain"/"My Love Belongs To You"	
4671	"It Feels So Nice"/"It Was So Nice While It Lasted"	1965

Stax
175	"I Take What I Want"/"Sweet Home"	1965
180	"You Don't Know Like I Know"/"Blame Me"	
189	"Hold On I'm A Comin' "/"I Got Everything I Need"	1966
198	"Said I Wasn't Gonna Tell Nobody"/"If You Got The Loving"	
204	"You Got Me Hummin' "/"Sleep Good Tonight"	
210	"When Something Is Wrong With My Baby"/ "Small Portion Of Your Love"	
218	"Soothe Me"/"I Can't Stand Up For Falling Down"	1967
231	"Soul Man"/"May I Baby"	
242	"I Thank You"/"Wrap It Up"	

Atlantic
2517	"You Don't Know What You Mean To Me"/ "This Is Your World"	1968

2540 "Can't You Find Another Way"/"Still Is The
     Night"
2568 "Everybody Got To Believe In Somebody"/"If
     I Didn't Have A Girl Like You"
2590 "Soul Sister Brown Sugar"/"Come On In"   1969
2608 "Born Again"/"Get It"
2668 "Ooh, Ooh, Ooh"/"Holdin' On"

NOTABLE MEMPHIS SOUND ARTISTS

Rufus Thomas

Several of the brighter Memphis sound stars began
recording in the early and mid-50's. Rufus Thomas, a longtime Memphis disc jockey, was without a doubt the king
of the 60's novelty dance record. His earliest Stax label hit
was the stuttering-tempo "Walkin' The Dog." All of Rufus
Thomas' Stax releases featured a strong blues feeling that
was perfect for his good-natured vocals.

Single Releases

Talent
  807 "I'm So Worried"/"I'll Be A Good Boy"   1950

Chess
 1466 "Night Walkin' Blues"/"Why Did You Dee   1952
     Gee"
 1492 "No More Doggin' Around"/"Crazy Bout"
 1517 "Juanita"/"Decorate The Counter"

Sun
  181 "Bearcat"/"Walkin' In The Rain"   1953
  188 "Tiger Man"/"Save That Money"

Meteor
 5039 "The Easy Livin' Plan"/"I'm Steady Holdin'   1957
     On"

Atco

6177	"Cause I Love You"/"Deep Down Inside" (with Carla Thomas)	1960
6199	"I Didn't Believe"/"Yeah, Yea-ah" (with Carla Thomas)	

Stax

126	"It's Aw-rite"/"Can't Ever Let You Go"	1962
130	"The Dog"/"Did You Ever Love A Woman"	1963
140	"Walking The Dog"/"Fine And Mellow"	
140	"Walking The Dog"/"You Said"	
144	"Can Your Monkey Do The Dog"/"I Want To Get Married"	
149	"Somebody Stole My Dog"/"I Want To Be Loved"	
151	"Night Time Is The Right Time"/"That's Really Some Good" (with Carla Thomas)	1964
157	"All Night Worker"/"Jump Back"	
167	"Little Sally Walker"/"Baby Walk"	1965
173	"Willy Nilly"/"Sho Gonna Mess Him Up"	
176	"When You Move You Lose"/"We're Tight" (with Carla Thomas)	
178	"Chicken Scratch"/"The World Is Round"	
184	"Never Let You Go"/"Birds And Bees" (with Carla Thomas)	1966
200	"Sister's Got A Boyfriend"/"Talkin' Bout True Love"	
221	"Greasy Spoon"/"Sophisticated Sissy"	1967
240	"Steady Holding On"/"Down Ta My House"	
250	"The Memphis Train"/"I Think I Made A Boo Boo"	1968
0010	"Funky Mississippi"/"So Hard To Get Along With"	
0022	"Funky Way"/"I Want To Hold You"	
0059	"Funky Chicken"/"Turn Your Damper Down"	1969
0071	"The Preacher And The Bear"/"Sixty Minute Man"	

Solomon Burke

Solomon Burke's earliest recordings were largely gospel material for the Apollo label. In 1961, Burke recorded the pop-flavored hit "Just Out Of Reach" and the bounce-tempo "Cry To Me." He then progressed into a more positive shouting style that resembled the approach of Wilson Pickett—this is especially evident in Burke's rendition of Pickett's "If You Need Me." Pickett responded by borrowing Burke's 1964 "Everybody Needs Somebody" for a 1967 hit. Solomon Burke's 1965 singles, "Got To Get You Off My Mind" and "Tonight's The Night" were successful at the mid-60's revitalization of Atlantic records.

Single Releases

Apollo

485	"Christmas Presents"/"When I'm All Alone"	1955
491	"I'm All Alone"/"To Thee"	1956
500	"No Man Walks Alone"/"Walking In A Dream"	
505	"You Can Run But You Can't Hide"/"A Picture Of You"	
511	"I Need You Tonight"/"This Is It"	1957
512	"For You And You Alone"/"You Are My Love"	
522	"They Always Say"/"Don't Cry"	1958
527	"My Heart Is A Chapel"/"This Is It"	

Atlantic

2089	"Keep The Magic Working"/"How Many Times"	1961
2114	"Just Out Of Reach"/"Be Bop Grandma"	
2131	"Cry To Me"/"I Almost Lost My Mind"	
2147	"I'm Hanging Up My Heart For You"/"Down In The Valley"	1962
2157	"I Really Don't Want To Know"/"Tonight My Heart She Is Crying"	

2170	"Go On Back To Him"/"I Said I Was Sorry"	1963
2180	"Words"/"Home In Your Heart"	
2185	"If You Need Me"/"You Can Make It If You Try"	
2196	"Can't Nobody Love You"/"Stupidity"	
2205	"You're Good For Me"/"Beautiful Brown Eyes"	
2218	"He'll Have To Go"/"Rockin' Soul"	1964
2226	"Goodbye Baby"/"Someone To Love Me"	
2241	"Everybody Needs Somebody To Love"/"Looking For My Baby"	
2254	"Yes I Do"/"Won't You Give Him"	
2259	"The Price"/"More Rockin' Soul"	
2276	"Got To Get You Off My Mind"/"Peepin'"	1965
2288	"Tonight's The Night"/"Maggie's Farm"	
2308	"Only Love"/"Little Girl That Loves Me"	
2314	"Baby Come On Home"/"Can't Stop Lovin' You Now"	
2345	"Lawdy Miss Claudy"/"Suddenly"	1966
2349	"Keep Looking"/"I Don't Want You No More"	
2359	"When She Touches Me"/"Woman How Do You Make Me Love You Like I Do"	
2369	"A Tear Fell"/"Presents For Christmas"	
2378	"Keep A Light In The Window Till I Come Home"/"Time Is A Thief"	1967
2459	"Detroit City"/"It's Been A Change"	
2507	"I Wish I Knew"/"It's Just A Matter Of Time"	
2537	"Meet Me In Church"/"Save It"	1968
2566	"What'd I Say"/"Get Out Of My Life Woman"	

Don Covay

Don Covay specialized in aggressive-beat, Southern-style material. Covay's "Mercy Mercy" on Rosemart and the more successful "See Saw" and "Sookie Sookie" on Atlantic are fine jolting rockers.

Single Releases

As by Pretty Boy:

Atlantic
1147   "Paper Dollar"/"Bip Bop Bip"   1957

As by Don Covay:

Sue
709   "Believe It Or Not"/"Betty Jean"   1959

Big
617   "Switchen In The Kitchen"/"Rockin' The   1959
Mule"

Columbia
41981   "Shake Wid The Snake"/"Every Which-A-   1961
Way"
42058   "See About Me"/"Hand Jive Workout"
42197   "Now That I Need You"/"Teen Life Swag"

Big Top
3060   "Hey There"/"I'm Coming Down With The
Blues"

Epic
9484   "It's Twistin' Time"/"Twistin' Train"   1962

Cameo
239   "The Popeye Waddle"/"One Little Boy Had   1962
Money"
251   "Wiggle Wobble"/"Do The Pug"

Arnold
1002   "Pony Time"/"Love Boat"   1962

Parkway
894   "Ain't That Silly"/"Turn It On"   1963
910   "The Froog"/"One Little Boy Had Money"   1964

Landa
701   "You're Good For Me"   1964

Rosemart
801   "Mercy Mercy"/"Can't Stay Away"   1964

802 "Take This Hurt Off Me"/"Please Don't Let
Me Know"

Atlantic
2280 "The Boomerang"/"Daddy Loves Baby" 1965
2286 "Please Do Something"/"A Woman's Love"
2301 "See Saw"/"I Never Get Enough Of Your
Love"
2323 "Sookie Sookie"/"Watching The Late Late 1966
Show"
2340 "Iron Out The Rough Spots"/"You Put
Something On Me"
2357 "Temptation Was Too Strong"/"Somebody's
Got To Love You"
2375 "Shingaling '67"/"I Was There" 1967
2407 "40 Days—40 Nights"/"The Usual Place"
2440 "You've Got Me On The Critical List"/"Never 1968
Had No Love"
2494 "It's In The Wind"/"Don't Let Go"
2521 "House On The Corner"/"Gonna Send You
Back To Your Mama"
2565 "I Stole Some Love"/"Snake In The Grass"
2609 "Sweet Pea"/"C.C. Rider Blues" 1969
2666 "Black Woman"/"Ice Cream Man"

Johnnie Taylor

Johnnie Taylor became a master of the slow blues vocal
with his early Stax label hits, "I Had A Dream" and "I Got
To Love Somebody's Baby." "Who's Making Love," a
hard-hitting rock record, dealt bluntly with extramarital
affairs and became a best-seller of 1968.

Single Releases

As by Johnnie Taylor:

Derby
101 "Dance What You Wanna"/"Shine Shine 1961
Shine"

1006 "In Love With You"/"Baby We've Got Love"

Sar

131	"Rome"/"Never Never"	1963
156	"Oh How I Love You"/"Run But You Can't Hide"	

Stax

186	"I Had A Dream"/"Changes"	1965
193	"I Got To Love Somebody's Baby"/"Just The One I've Been Looking For"	1966
202	"Little Bluebird"/"Toe Hold"	
209	"Ain't That Loving You"/"Outside Love"	
226	"If I Had It To Do Over"/"You Can't Get Away From It"	1967
235	"Somebody's Sleeping In My Bed"/"Strange Things"	
253	"I Ain't Particular"/"Where There's Smoke There's Fire"	1968
0009	"Who's Making Love"/"I'm Trying"	
0023	"Take Care Of Your Homework"/"Hold On This Time"	
0033	"Testify"/"I Had A Fight With Love"	
0042	"Just Keep On Loving Me"/"My Life" (with Carla Thomas)	
0046	"I Could Never Be President"/"It's Amazing"	1969
0055	"Love Bones"/"Mr. Nobody Is Somebody"	
0068	"Steal Away"/"Friday Night"	

As by Johnnie Taylor, William Bell, Pervis Staples, Eddie Floyd, Carla Thomas, Mavis Staples, C. Staples with Isaac Hayes:

Stax

0040	"Soul-A-Lujah"/"Soul-A-Lujah" (instr.)	1969

Eddie Floyd

Eddie Floyd began his singing career with the same 50's Falcons' vocal group that produced Wilson Pickett.

Floyd's 1966 release "Knock On Wood" was a pulsating medium-tempo effort and an early Stax records hit.

Single Releases

Lupine
1022	"A Deed To Your Heart"/"I'll Be Home"	1964

Safice
334	"Never Get Enough Of Your Love"/"Baby Bye"	1964
338	"Make Up Your Mind"/"No No No"	1965

Atlantic
2275	"Drive On"/"Hush Hush"	1965

Stax
187	"Things Get Better"/"Good Love Bad Love"	1965
194	"Knock On Wood"/"Got To Make A Comeback"	1966
208	"Raise Your Hand"/"I've Just Been Feeling Bad"	
219	"Don't Rock The Boat"/"This House"	1967
223	"Love Is A Doggone Good Thing"/"Hey Now"	
233	"On A Saturday Night"/"Under My Nose"	
246	"Holding On With Both Hands"/"Big Bird"	1968
0002	"I've Never Found A Girl (To Love Me Like You Do)"/"I'm Just The Kind Of Fool"	
0012	"Bring It On Home To Me"/"Sweet Things You Do"	
0025	"I've Got To Have Your Love"/"Girl I Love You"	
0036	"Don't Tell Your Mama"/"Consider Me"	
0041	"Never Never Let You Go"/"Ain't That Good" (with Mavis Staples)	1969
0051	"Why Is The Wine Sweeter (On The Other Side)"/"People Get It Together"	
0060	"California Girl"/"Woodman"	

Arthur Conley

Arthur Conley had one major hit, the high-velocity "Sweet Soul Music," which was a tribute to several rhythm and blues singing stars from a 1966 perspective. Later ballad performances by Arthur Conley reflect a strong Sam Cooke influence.

Single Releases

Jotis

470	"I'm A Lonely Stranger"/"Where He Leads Me"	1965
472	"Who's Fooling Who"	

Fame

1009	"I'm Gonna Forget About You"/"Take Me"	1965

Atco

6463	"Sweet Soul Music"/' Let's Go Steady"	1966
6494	"Shake Rattle And Roll"/"You Don't Have To See Me"	1967
6529	"Whole Lotta Woman"/"Love Comes And Goes"	
6563	"Funky Street"/ 'Put Our Love Together"	1968
6588	"People Sure Act Funny"/"Burning Fire"	
6622	"Aunt Dora's Love Soul Shack"/"Is That You Love"	
6640	"Ob-La-Di-Ob-La-Da"/' Otis Sleep On"	1969
6661	"Speak Her Name"/"Run On"	

Clarence Carter

Clarence Carter's major hit was the 1968 ballad, "Slip Away." The Carter voice has a fine emotional edge, but no later release was a major hit.

Single Releases

Fame
1010	"Tell Daddy"	1966
1013	"Thread The Needle"/"Don't Make My Baby Cry"	
1016	"The Road Of Love"/"She Ain't Gonna Do Right"	

Atlantic
2461	"Looking For A Fox"	1967
2508	"Slip Away"/"Funky Fever"	1968
2569	"Too Weak To Fight"/' Let Me Comfort You"	
2576	"Back Door Santa"	
2605	"Snatching It Back"/"Making Love"	1969
2642	"The Feeling Is Right"/"You Can't Miss What You Can't Measure"	
2660	"Doin' Our Thing"/"I Smell A Rat"	

Percy Sledge

Percy Sledge's first release was the understated responsive ballad, "When A Man Loves A Woman." "Take Time To Know Her" was similarly expressive with appropriately melancholy lyrics.

Single Releases

Atlantic
2326	"When A Man Loves A Woman"/"Love Me Like You Mean It"	1966
2342	"Warm And Tender Love"/"Sugar Puddin'"	
2358	"It Tears Me Up"/"Heart Of A Child"	
2383	"Baby Help Me"/"You've Got That Something Wonderful"	
2396	"Out Of Left Field"/"It Can't Be Stopped"	1967
2414	"What Am I Living For"/"Love Me Tender"	

2434   "Just Out Of Reach"/"Hard To Believe"
2453   "Cover Me"/"Behind Every Great Man
          There's A Woman"
2490   "Take Time To Know Her"/"It's All Wrong   1968
          But It's Alright"
2539   "Sudden Stop"/"Between These Arms"
2563   "You're All Around Me"
2594   "My Special Prayer"/"Bless Your Little Sweet
          Soul"
2616   "Any Day Now"/"The Angels Listened In"   1969
2646   "Kind Woman"/"Woman Of The Night"

The Sweet Inspirations

The Sweet Inspirations possessed a satisfying rich vocal
sound that was perfect for their major hit, "Sweet Inspiration." The Inspirations also provided a full background
sound to several Memphis sound hits.

Single Releases

Atlantic
2410   "Why"/"I Don't Want To Go On Without   1967
          You"
2418   "When Something Is Wrong With My Baby"/
          "Let It Be Me"
2436   "That's How Strong My Love Is"/"I've Been
          Loving You Too Long"
2449   "Don't Fight It"/"Oh What A Fool I've Been"
2465   "Do Right Woman Do Right Man"/"Reach
          Out For Me"
2476   "Sweet Inspiration"/"I'm Blue"   1968
2529   "To Love Somebody"/"Where Did It Go"
2551   "Unchained Melody"/"Am I Ever Going To
          See My Baby Again"
2571   "You Really Didn't Mean It"/"What The
          World Needs Now Is Love"

2620 "Everyday Will Be Like A Holiday"/"Crying 1969
In The Rain"
2638 "Sweets For My Sweet"/"Get A Little Order"
2653 "Chained"/"Don't Go"
2686 "A Brand New Lover Pt. 1 & 2"

Rock

and

Roll

Rock Music

Rock and roll music of the early 60's, an extension of
50's rock and roll, evolved into rock and hard rock
in the post-1966 era. The next several sections will
trace this emerging style by discussing the approaches
and recordings of important 60's rock and roll artists
and rock groups. Also, in those few specific areas
where 60's recordings are unusually valuable, I will
discuss scarcity and value.

EARLY 60'S ROCK AND ROLL ARTISTS

•

Rockabilly music did not carry over into the 60's as well as rhythm and blues music did. A highly disproportionate number of the cream of 50's rockabilly talent met with tragedy at the very end of the decade. Death was the fate of Buddy Holly, Eddie Cochran, Ritchie Valens and J.P. Richardson (The Big Bopper); Carl Perkins' near-fatal injuries and Gene Vincent's poor health temporarily interrupted these two great recording careers. Even in the volatile world of rock and roll music, this was an extremely high toll of extraordinary talent. Undoubtedly, had circumstances been different, these classic rock and roll performers would have remained solid and effective in the 60's and continued to profoundly influence rock.

Instead, early rockabilly-derived recording talent was diffused during the early 60's. Of the original Sun records rockabilly roster, only Elvis Presley and Roy Orbison continued to record with any impact. The simplicity and force of Sun rockabilly was lost in favor of more professionally produced rock and roll. Elvis became immersed in pop material, while Roy Orbison recorded rock and roll of a decidedly gloomy character. Others—including Jerry Lee Lewis, Conway Twitty and Jack Scott—became headline country and western recording artists who little benefited the growth of early 60's rock and roll.

Elvis Presley

Elvis Presley, the original rock and roll superstar, entered the 60's decade with some very successful, glossily produced ballads—"Are You Lonesome Tonight," "Can't Help Falling In Love" and the mildly up-tempo "Surrender." Interspersed among these most professionally rendered love songs were several hard-hitting rock and roll single releases—most notably "I Feel So Bad" and "Little Sister," both with prominent guitar work. By the mid-60's, with the emergence of British and soul-pop, Elvis Presley's single releases took on a shallow quality with such forgettably faddish titles as "Bossa Nova Baby," "Viva Las Vegas," "Do The Clam" and "Spinout." Elvis Presley did have some best-selling singles during this 1963–1967 time period, mostly with such solid rhythm and blues material as "Love Letters," "Crying In The Chapel" and "Such A Night." The latter two were 50's classics. In 1968, Elvis Presley returned to recording original titles that suited his fine rock and roll talents. He came on strong with "Guitar Man" and the likable "U.S. Male." During this latter part of the 60's, Elvis Presley's biggest hit was the sensitively rendered "In The Ghetto," the forerunner of two other social statements—"Clean Up Your Own Backyard" and the enormously successful "Suspicious Minds."

Single Releases

Sun

209	"That's All Right"/"Blue Moon Of Kentucky" (also on RCA 6380)	1954
210	"Good Rockin' Tonight"/"I Don't Care If The Sun Don't Shine" (also on RCA 6381)	
215	"Milkcow Blues Boogie"/"You're A Heartbreaker" (also on RCA 6382)	1955
217	"Baby Let's Play House"/"I'm Left, You're Right She's Gone" (also on RCA 6383)	

223 "Mystery Train"/"I Forgot To Remember To Forget" (also on RCA 6357)

RCA

6420	"Heartbreak Hotel"/"I Was The One"	1956
6540	"I Want You, I Need You, I Love You"/"My Baby Left Me"	
6604	"Hound Dog"/"Don't Be Cruel"	
6636	"Blue Suede Shoes"/"Tutti Frutti"	1956
6637	"I Got A Woman"/"I'm Countin' On You"	
6638	"I'm Gonna Sit Right Down And Cry"/"I'll Never Let You Go"	
6639	"Tryin' To Get To You"/"I Love You Because"	
6640	"Just Because"/"Blue Moon"	
6641	"Money Honey"/"One-Sided Love Affair"	
6642	"Shake Rattle And Roll"/"Lawdy Miss Clawdy"	
6643	"Love Me Tender"/"Anyway You Want Me"	
6800	"Too Much"/"Playing For Keeps"	1957
6870	"All Shook Up"/"That's When Your Heartaches Begin"	
7000	"Teddy Bear"/"Loving You"	
7035	"Jailhouse Rock"/"Treat Me Nice"	
7150	"I Beg Of You"/"Don't"	
7240	"Wear My Ring Around Your Neck"/"Doncha Think It's Time"	1958
7280	"Hard-Headed Woman"/"Don't Ask Me Why"	
7410	"One Night"/"I Got Stung"	
7506	"A Fool Such As I"/"I Need Your Love Tonight"	1959
7600	"A Big Hunk O' Love"/"My Wish Came True"	
7740	"Stuck On You"/"Fame And Fortune"	1960
7777	"It's Now Or Never"/"A Mess Of Blues"	
7810	"Are You Lonesome Tonight"/"I Gotta Know"	
7850	"Surrender"/"Lonely Man"	1961
7880	"I Feel So Bad"/"Wild In The Country"	
7908	"Little Sister"/"His Latest Flame"	
7968	"Can't Help Falling In Love"/"Rock-A-Hula Baby"	

7992 "Good Luck Charm"/"Anything That's Part   1962
      Of You"
8041 "She's Not You"/"Just Tell Her Jim Said
      Hello"
8100 "Return To Sender"/"Where Do You Come
      From"
8134 "One Broken Heart For Sale"/"They Remind   1963
      Me Too Much Of You"
8188 "(You're The) Devil In Disguise"/"Please
      Don't Drag That String Again"
8243 "Bossa Nova Baby"/"Witchcraft"
8307 "Kissin' Cousins"/"It Hurts Me"
0639 "Kiss Me Quick"/"Suspicion"   1964
8360 "Viva Las Vegas"/"What'd I Say"
8400 "Such A Night"/"Never Ending"
8440 "Ain't That Loving You Baby"/"Ask Me"
0720 "Blue Christmas"/"Wooden Heart"
8500 "Do The Clam"/"You'll Be Gone"   1965
0643 "Crying In The Chapel"/"I Believe In The
      Man In The Sky"
8585 "Easy Question"/"It Feels So Right"
8657 "I'm Yours"/"Long Lonely Highway"
0647 "Blue Christmas"/"Santa Claus Is Back In
      Town"
0650 "Puppet On A String"/"Wooden Heart"
8740 "Tell Me Why"/"Blue River"   1966
0651 "Joshua Fit The Battle"/"Known Only To
      Him"
0652 "Milky White Way"/"Swing Down Sweet
      Chariot"
8780 "Frankie And Johnny"/"Please Don't Stop
      Loving Me"
8870 "Love Letters"/"Come What May"
8941 "Spinout"/"All That I Am"
8950 "If Every Day Was Like Chritsmas"/"How
      Would You Like To Be"
9056 "Indescribably Blue"/"Fools Fall In Love"   1967
9115 "Long Legged Girl"/"That's Someone You
      Never Forget"

9287	"There's Always Me"/"Judy"	
9341	"Big Boss Man"/"You Don't Know Me"	
9425	"Guitar Man"/"High Heel Sneakers"	1968
9465	"U.S. Male"/"Stay Away Joe"	
9547	"Let Yourself Go"/"Your Time Hasn't Come Yet Baby"	
9600	"You'll Never Walk Alone"/"We Call On Him"	
9610	"A Little Less Conversation"/"Almost In Love"	
9670	"If I Can Dream"/"Edge Of Reality"	
9731	"Memories"/"Charro"	1969
0130	"How Great Thou Art"/"His Hand In Mine"	
9741	"In The Ghetto"/"Any Day Now"	
9747	"Clean Up Your Own Backyard"/"The Fair Is Moving On"	
9764	"Suspicious Minds"/"You'll Think Of Me"	
9768	"Don't Cry Daddy"/"Rubberneckin'"	
9791	"Kentucky Rain"/"My Little Friend"	

Roy Orbison

Originally with Sun records during the mid-50's, Roy Orbison was able to inject a Southern rockabilly feeling into his early 60's Monument label recordings. Orbison's material tended to dwell on such downbeat themes as loneliness, rejected love and contemplated suicide, and his voice, inflections and vocal approach were natural and effective with these melancholy themes. The overriding impact of such hits as "Crying," "Runnin' Scared" and "Leah" is gloom and deep depression. Roy Orbison's first major 60's hit, "Only The Lonely," was rendered in a haunting up-tempo. Other hits included such rock and roll releases as "I'm Hurtin'," "Dream Baby" and his biggest hit, the classic "Oh Pretty Woman." Roy Orbison also recorded some fine, Southern-style blues, such as "Candy Man" and "Mean Woman Blues."

Single Releases

As by The Teen Kings:

Jewel

101	"Ooby Dooby"/"Go Go Go"	1955

As by Roy Orbison:

Sun

242	"Ooby Dooby"/"Go Go Go"	1956
251	"You're My Baby"/"Rockhouse"	
265	"Sweet And Easy"/"Devil Doll"	1957
	(also on Sun 353)	
284	"Chicken Hearted"/"I Like Love"	

RCA

7381	"Sweet And Innocent"/"Seems To Me"	1958
7447	"Almost Eighteen"/"Jolie"	

Monument

409	"Paper Boy"/"With The Bug"	1959
412	"Uptown"/"Pretty One"	1960
421	"Only The Lonely"/"Here Comes That Song Again"	
425	"Blue Angel"/"Today's Teardrops"	
433	"I'm Hurtin' "/"I Can't Stop Loving You"	
438	"Runnin' Scared"/"Love Hurts"	1961
447	"Candy Man"/"Crying"	
456	"Dream Baby"/"The Actress"	1962
461	"The Crowd"/"Mama"	
467	"Leah"/"Workin' For The Man"	
806	"In Dreams"/"Shaddaroba"	1963
815	"Falling"/"Distant Drums"	
824	"Mean Woman Blues"/"Blue Bayou"	
830	"Pretty Paper"/"Beautiful Dreamer"	
837	"It's Over"/"Indian Wedding"	1964
851	"Oh Pretty Woman"/"Yo Te Amo Maria"	
873	"Goodnight"/"Only With You"	1965
891	"Say You're My Girl"/"Sleepy Hollow"	

906 "Let The Good Times Roll"/"Distant Drums"
939 "Lana"/"Our Summer Song"

The Band

As The Hawks, with a Ronnie Hawkins lead, this Canadian group performed effective, no-nonsense rock and roll. Among their hits were the rhythm-and-blues derived "Mary Lou"—a Young Jesse original (Modern 961)—and "Ruby Baby"—a Drifters original. Subsequent aggressive vocal releases by Hawkins and The Hawks were not best-sellers. By 1965, The Hawks had become Levon and The Hawks on two obscure Atco label releases. The group finally reached rock importance as The Band. After providing backup work for Bob Dylan, The Band had two major hits, "The Weight" and "Up On Cripple Creek." Though they were titles original to The Band, these and subsequent single releases had the truthful-ringing lyrical content and power of longtime folk classics.

Single Releases

As by Ronnie Hawkins and The Hawks:

Quality
6128 "Hey Bo Diddley"/"Love Me Like You Can"   1958

Roulette
4154 "Forty Days"/"One Of These Days"   1959
4177 "Mary Lou"/"Need Your Lovin'"
4209 "Southern Love"/"Love Me Like You Can"   1960
4228 "Lonely Hours"/"Clara"
4231 "Ballad Of Carly Chessman"/"Tale Of Lloyd Collins"
4249 "Ruby Baby"/"Hay Ride"   1961
4267 "Summertime"/"Mister And Mississippi"

4311   "Cold Cold Heart"/"Nobody's Lonesome For   1962
       Me"
4400   "Come Love"/"I Feel Good"
4483   "Bo Diddley"/"Who Do You Love"   1963
4502   "High Blood Pressure"/"There's A Screw
       Loose"

As by Levon and The Hawks:

Atco
6383   "The Stones I Throw"/"He Don't Love You"   1965
6625   "Go Go Lisa Jane"/"He Don't Love You"   1968

As by The Band:

Capitol
2269   "The Weight"/"I Shall Be Released"   1968
2635   "Up On Cripple Creek"/"The Night They   1969
       Drove Old Dixie Down"

NOTABLE EARLY 60'S ROCK AND ROLL ARTISTS

Sir Douglas Quintet

Originally known as Doug Sahm and The Markays, Sir Douglas Quintet was an early Texas rock and roll group. One early Sir Douglas hit was the shuffle-beat "She's About A Mover."

Single Releases

As by Doug Sahm and The Markays:

Harlem
107   "Why Oh Why"/"If You Ever Need Me"   1960
      (also on Swingin' 625)

As by Doug Sahm and The Spirits:

Personality
    3505   "Crazy Crazy Feeling"/"Baby What's On
              Your Mind" (also on Renner 215)   ca. 1960

Renner
    212   "Big Hat"/"Makes No Difference"   ca. 1960
    226   "Just Because"/"Two Hearts In Love"

As by Sir Douglas Quintet:

Tribe
    8308   "She's About A Mover"/"We'll Take Our Last 1965
           Walk Tonight"
    8310   "Blue Norther"/"The Tracker"
    8312   "In Time"/"The Story Of John Hardy"
    8314   "The Rains Came"/"Bacon Fat"
    8317   "Quarter To 3"/"She's Gotta Be Boss"   1966
    8318   "Beginning Of The End"/"Love Don't Treat
           Me Fair"
    8321   "She Digs My Love"/"When I Sing The
           Blues"

Smash
    2169   "Are Inlaws Really Outlaws"/"Honky Blues" 1968
    2191   "Mendocino"/"I Wanna Be Your Mama   1969
           Again"
    2222   "It Didn't Even Bring Me Down"/"Lawd I'm
           Just A Country Boy In The Great Big
           Freaky City"
    2233   "Dynamite Woman"/"Too Many Prociled
           Minds"
    2253   "At The Crossroads"
    2259   "Nuevo Laredo"

Sam the Sham

Sam the Sham, a second Texas rock and roll group, did enormously well with a string of novelty hits. Their primitive "Wooly Bully" and their tongue-in cheek "Lil Red Riding Hood" were both number one hits.

Single Releases

Tupelo
2982	"Betty And Dupree"/"Man Child"	1963

Dingo
001	"Haunted House"/"How Does A Cheating Woman Feel"	1964

XL
905	"The Signifyin' Monkey"/"Juimonos"	1964

MGM
13322	"Wooly Bully"/"Ain't Gonna Move"	1965
13364	"Ju Ju Hand"/"Bright City Lights"	
13397	"Ring Dang Doo"/"Don't Try It"	
13452	"Red Hot"/"Long Long Way"	1966
13506	"Lil Red Riding Hood"/"Love Me Like Before"	
13581	"The Hair On My Chinny Chin Chin"/"The Out Crowd"	
13649	"How Do You Catch A Girl"/"The Love You Left Behind"	
13713	"Oh That's Good, No That's Bad"/"Take What You Can Get"	1967
13747	"Black Sheep"/"My Day's Gonna Come"	
13803	"Banned In Boston"/"Money's My Problem"	
13863	"Yakety Yak"/"Let Our Love Light Shine"	
13920	"Old MacDonald Had A Boogaloo Farm"	1968
13972	"I Couldn't Spell It!!*!"/"The Down-Home Strut"	

FOLK ROCK

•

Folk rock emerged on record in the mid-60's when it was often performed by Greenwich Village based performers. Bob Dylan was the moving force; his material and style proved deeply influential. Folk rock, an offshoot of folk music, lost some of the gentle innocence of folk music and became instead a medium of protest, often with acidic lyrics.

Folk Rock Scarcity and Value

Certain early Bob Dylan single releases, especially the initial Columbia label single, have recently attracted demand and prices in the $5 range are common. The Neil Diamond single on Columbia is also scarce and valued over $2. The predecessors to Simon and Garfunkle, the Tom and Jerry singles, are valued in the $5 area. The original issue of "Get Together" by The Youngbloods is much scarcer than the reissue and is valued in the $2 range.

Bob Dylan

Bob Dylan—also known as Blind Boy Grunt, among other early pseudonyms—originally performed classic blues material. His first Columbia singles were of his own folk compositions—the best known was his own poetically rendered "Blowin' In The Wind" with the biting flip, "Don't Think Twice It's Alright." This seed of satire was more evident in the revolutionary-themed "Subterranean Homesick Blues." Dylan's acoustic folk releases soon gave way to electric folk rock with "Like A Rolling Stone" and the expertly derisive "Positively 4th Street." "Rainy Day Women #12 & 35" is an extended drug expression. Bob Dylan refrained from issuing single releases after 1967 until his 1969 return, which was characterized by the softer, more sympathetic approach of "Lay Lady Lay" and "Tonight I'll Be Staying Here With You." From the idealism of his early 60's protest expressions, through his strident mid-60's electric rock to the mild, countrified ballads at the decade's end, Bob Dylan decisively influenced rock throughout the 60's.

Single Releases

Columbia

42856	"Blowin' In The Wind"/"Don't Think Twice It's Alright"	1963
43242	"Subterranean Homesick Blues"/"She Belongs to Me"	1965
43346	"Like A Rolling Stone"/"Gates Of Eden"	
43389	"Positively 4th Street"/"From A Buick 6"	
43477	"Highway 61 Revisited"/"Can You Please Crawl Out Your Window"	
43541	"One Of Us Must Know"/"Queen Jane Approximately"	1966
43592	"Rainy Day Women #12 & 35"/"Pledging My Time"	
43683	"I Want You"/"Just Like Tom Thumb's Blues"	
43792	"Just Like A Woman"/"Obviously 5 Believers"	
44069	"Leopard Skin Pill-Box Hat"/"Most Likely You'll Go Your Way And I'll Go Mine"	1967

44826	"I Threw It All Away"/"Drifter's Escape"	1969
44926	"Lay Lady Lay"/"Peggy Day"	
45004	"Tonight I'll Be Staying Here With You"/ "Country Pie"	

Neil Diamond

A consistently satisfying artist, Neil Diamond represents a dominant trend in the popularization of rock music. Neil Diamond's early releases were a combination of the folk ballad, "Solitary Man," with some engaging, spritely rock and roll, "Cherry, Cherry" and the good-natured "I Thank The Lord For The Night Time." Diamond's early releases were in fact remarkable expressions of good times, symbolizing this aspect of the 60's life style. Woven throughout Neil Diamond's music is a sensuality that was strongly projected in his later, more sophisticated ballads, "Sweet Caroline" and "Holly Holly"—both major hits. Neil Diamond, both as a composer and as a performer, is one of the brighter stars to emerge in the mid and late-60's.

Single Releases

Columbia

42809	"Clown Town"/"At Night"	1963

Bang

519	"Solitary Man"/"Do It"	1966
528	"Cherry Cherry"/"I'll Come Running"	
536	"I Got The Feelin' Oh No No"/"The Boat I Row"	
540	"You Got To Me"/"Someday Baby"	1967
542	"Girl You'll Be A Woman Soon"/"You'll Forget"	
547	"I Thank The Lord For The Night Time"/"The Long Way Home"	

551 "Kentucky Woman"/"The Time Is Now"
554 "New Orleans"/"Hanky Panky"
556 "Red Red Wine"/"Red Rubber Ball"   1968
561 "Shilo"/"La Bamba"

Uni

55065 "Brooklyn Roads"/"Holiday Inn"   1968
55075 "Two Bit Manchild"/"Broad Old Woman"
55084 "Sunday Sun"/"Honey Drippin' Times"   1969
55109 "Brother Love's Travelling Salvation Show"
55136 "Sweet Caroline"/"Dig In"
55175 "Holly Holly"/"Hurtin' You Don't Come Easy"

Simon and Garfunkle

While known as Tom and Jerry, the duo had a little-known 1959 release—the novelty "Hey Schoolgirl," performed in a strong up-tempo Everly Brothers' style. With the mid-60's folk rock resurgence, the poetic recordings by Simon and Garfunkle were quickly and widely acclaimed. In fact, much of the accessibility of the Tom and Jerry release carried over into the lyrically stronger Simon and Garfunkle recordings. "I Am A Rock" and "A Hazy Lazy Shade Of Winter" were both very friendly, pleasant releases. A wistful melancholy is evident in the excellent mood-setting performances "Homeward Bound" and "Scarborough Fair." Simon and Garfunkle's major hit was the rhythmic "Mrs. Robinson."

Single Releases

As by Tom and Jerry:

Big

613 "Hey Schoolgirl"/"Dancin' Wild"   1959
616 "Our Song"

Hunt
 319 "That's My Story"   1959

As by Simon and Garfunkle:

Columbia
43396	"Sounds Of Silence"/"We've Got A Groovey Thing Goin'"	1965
43511	"Homeward Bound"/"Leaves That Are Green"	1966
43617	"I Am A Rock"/"Flowers Never Bend With The Rainfall"	
43728	"Dangling Conversation"/"The Big Bright Green Pleasure Machine"	
43873	"A Hazy Lazy Shade Of Winter"/"For Emily Whenever I May Find Her"	
44232	"Fakin' It"/"You Don't Know Where Your Interest Lies"	1967
44404	"At The Zoo"/"The 59th Street Bridge Song"	
44465	"Scarborough Fair"/"April Come She Will"	1968
44511	"Mrs. Robinson"/"Old Friends/Bookends"	
44785	"The Boxer"/"Baby Driver"	1969
45079	"Bridge Over Troubled Water"/"Keep The Customer Satisfied"	

The Byrds

The Byrds were the earliest successful Los Angeles folk rock group. The first two hit releases by The Byrds were the Bob Dylan compositions, "Mr. Tambourine Man" and the satirical "All I Really Want To Do." Both were ideal material for this low-energy group. Their early recordings were soaring, easily executed rock and roll that occasionally lacked excitement and emotional impact. But The Byrds' confident skill with contemporary material kept them popular. Losing some popularity in the very late 60's, The Byrds' sound took on a country and western feel, apparent in the delightful "You Ain't Going Nowhere."

Single Releases

As by The Beefeaters:

Elektra
45013   "Please Let Me Love You"/"Don't Be Long"   1964

As by The Byrds:

Columbia
43271   "Mr. Tambourine Man"/"I Knew I'd Want You"   1965

43332   "All I Really Want To Do"/"I'll Feel A Whole Lot Better"

43424   "She Don't Care About Time"/"Turn Turn Turn"

43501   "Set You Free This Time"/"It Won't Be Wrong"   1966

43578   "Eight Miles High"/"Why"

43702   "5D"/"Captain Soul"

43766   "Mr. Spaceman"/"What's Happening"

43987   "So You Want To Be A Rock N Roll Star"/"Everybody's Been Burned"   1967

44054   "My Back Pages"/"Renaissance Fair"

44157   "Have You Seen Her Face"/"Don't Make Waves"

44230   "Lady Friend"/"Old John Robertson"

44362   "Goin' Back"/"Change Is Now"   1968

44499   "You Ain't Going Nowhere"/"Artificial Energy"

44746   "Bad Night At The Whiskey"/"Drug Store Truck Drivin' Man"   1969

44868   "Lay Lady Lay"/"Old Blue"

44990   "Ballad Of Easy Rider"/"Oil In My Lamp"

NOTABLE NEW YORK ROCK AND
FOLK ROCK GROUPS

The Lovin' Spoonful

The Lovin' Spoonful combined friendly original lyrics with good-time jug-band rock and roll in the hit, "Do You Believe In Magic." The flip to this was the bluesy "On The Road Again." Also of a blues flavor was "Night Owl Blues," while the later "Summer In The City" was a shouting performance.

Single Releases

Kama Sutra

201	"Do You Believe In Magic"/"On The Road Again"	1965
205	"You Didn't Have To Be So Nice"/"My Gal"	
208	"Daydream"/"Night Owl Blues"	1966
209	"Did You Ever Have To Make Up Your Mind"/"Didn't Want To Have To Do It"	
211	"Summer In The City"/"Fishin' Blues"	
211	"Summer In The City"/"Butchie's Tune"	
216	"Rain On The Roof"/"Pow"	
219	"Nashville Cats"/"Full Measure"	1967
220	"Darling Be Home Soon"/"Darling Companion"	
225	"Six O'Clock"/"You're A Big Boy Now"	
231	"Lonely (Amy's Theme)"/"You're A Big Boy Now"	1968
239	"She Is Still A Mystery"/"Only Pretty What A Pity"	
241	"Money"/"Close Your Eyes"	
250	"Never Going Back"/"Forever"	
251	"Revelation: Revolution 69"/"Run With You"	1969
255	"Me About You"/"Amazing Air"	

The Youngbloods

The Youngbloods had one exceptional rockabilly-based

single "Grizzly Bear." The Youngbloods' "Get Together" had an enormous impact; a second-time-around hit during 1968–1969, "Get Together" developed into a 60s' anthem of unity.

Single Releases

RCA

9015	"Grizzly Bear"/"Tears Are Falling"	1966
9142	"Merry Go Round"/"Foolin' Around"	1967
9222	"Euphoria"/"The Wine Song"	
9264	"Get Together"/"All My Dreams Blue"	
9360	"Fool Me"/"I Can Tell"	
9422	"Quicksand"/"Dreamer's Dream"	1968
9752	"Get Together"/"Beautiful"	
0129	"Darkness, Darkness"/"On Sir Francis Drake"	1969
0270	"Sunlight"/"Trillium"	

Blood, Sweat and Tears

Blood, Sweat and Tears drew upon some early 60's soul music compositions and some original material, then added a full-blown rock instrumental sound and came up with the hits, "You've Made Me So Very Happy" and the shouting-blues "Spinning Wheel."

Single Releases

Columbia

44559	"I Can't Quit Her"/"House In The Country"	1968
44776	"You've Made Me So Very Happy"/"Blues Pt. 1"	1969
44871	"Spinning Wheel"/"More And More"	
45008	"And When I Die"/"Sometimes In Winter"	

EARLY CALIFORNIA ROCK AND ROLL

•

Early Los Angeles rock and roll was performed in several distinct forms: the surf-rock of The Beach Boys, Dick Dale and The Del-Tones and twenty or thirty mainly instrumental groups; the "blue-eyed soul" of The Righteous Brothers; and the gospel-blues of The Chambers Brothers. Two Bay Area groups, The Golliwogs—later known as The Creedence Clearwater Revival—and Sly and The Family Stone, recorded early 60's rock and roll and later 60's rock.

Scarcity and Value

The X label Beach Boys recording has brought as much as $50 at record auctions. The single is scarce as it was distributed only in the Los Angeles area, but a truer worth is closer to between $15 and $20. The Candix reissue of "Surfin'" brings around $5. Also in the $5 to $10 range are the pre-Creedence Clearwater singles by The Blue Velvets and The Golliwogs and singles issued by Sylvester Steward and by Sly.

The Beach Boys

The original and definitive surf-rock group was The Beach Boys, who recorded some of the best-known and

176

best-selling early 60's rock and roll. The Beach Boys first release "Surfin' " was not only good rock and roll, it also created the "surfin'/California sun/hot rod" school of popular music. The Beach Boys recorded some of the best-written and most professionally performed songs in the surf-rock form. These include the rockers "Surfin' Safari" and "Surfin' U.S.A." and the ballads "Surfer Girl" and "In My Room." Simultaneously, The Beach Boys were singing their own fine "hot rod" compositions—"409," "Shut Down" and "Little Deuce Coupe." Performances by The Beach Boys are extremely tight, pleasant and ingeniously harmonic, but they maintain the exciting feel of rock and roll. Songs like "Help Me Rhonda," "I Get Around," "Darlin" and especially "Good Vibrations" exemplify fine harmony and are 60's rock and roll classics.

Single Releases

As by The Beach Boys:

X
| 301 | "Surfin' "/"Luau" (also on Candix 301) | 1962 |

Capitol
4777	"Surfin' Safari"/"409"	
4880	"Ten Little Indians"/"County Fair" (also on Capitol 6060)	1963
4932	"Surfin' U.S.A."/"Shut Down"	
5009	"Surfer Girl"/"Little Deuce Coupe" "Boogie Woogie"/"Spirit Of America" (issue on the Capitol Custom label as a "Special Music City—KFWB Promotional Souvenir Copy")	
5069	"Be True To Your School"/"In My Room"	
5096	"Little Saint Nick"/"The Lord's Prayer"	
5118	"Fun Fun Fun"/"Why Do Fools Fall In Love"	1964
5174	"I Get Around"/"Don't Worry Baby"	

5245	"When I Grow Up"/"She Knows Me Too Well"	
5267	"Little Honda"/"Wendy/Hushabye/Don't Look Back"	
5306	"Dance Dance Dance"/"The Warmth Of The Sun"	
5312	"The Man With All The Toys"/"Blue Christmas"	
5372	"Do You Wanna Dance"/"Please Let Me Wonder"	1965
5395	"Help Me Rhonda"/"Kiss Me Baby"	
5464	"California Girls"/"Let Him Run Wild"	
5540	"Little Girl I Once Knew"/"There's No Other"	
5561	"Barbara Ann"/"Girl Don't Tell Me"	
5602	"Sloop John B"/"You're So Good To Me"	1966

As by Brian Wilson:

Capitol

5610	"Caroline No"/"Summer Means New Love"	1966

As by The Beach Boys:

Capitol

5676	"Good Vibrations"/"Let's Go Away For Awhile"	1966
5706	"God Only Knows"/"Wouldn't It Be Nice"	
2028	"Wild Honey"/"Wind Chimes"	1967
2068	"Darlin' "/"Here Today"	
2160	"Friends"/"Little Bird"	1968
2239	"Do It Again"/"Wake The World"	
2360	"Bluebirds Over The Mountain"/"Never Learn Not To Love"	
2432	"I Can Hear Music"/"All I Want To Do"	1969
2530	"Break Away"/"Celebrate The News"	

Brother

1001	"Heroes And Villains"/"You're Welcome"	1967
1002	"Gettin' Hungry"/"Devoted To You"	

NOTABLE SURF-ROCK ARTISTS

The surf-rock instrumental was the innovation of small obscure record labels. Often the masters were purchased and released by larger labels, especially Dot records, and only then did the releases develop major hit status.

Several of these recording studios were essentially back-room recording studios—such as Downey Music in Downey, California—where several of the best and most influential surf-rock instrumentals were produced. *The Chantays* and *The Rumblers* both featured a strong drum and guitar beat in their most popular recordings.

Single Releases

By The Rumblers:

Downey
    103   "Boss"/"I Don't Need You No More"   1962
         (also on Dot 16421)

By The Chantays:

Downey
    104   "Pipeline"/"Move It"   1962
         (also on Dot 16440)

The Rockin' Rebels

A few of the best early rock instrumentals were produced on the East Coast and in the Midwest, most significantly "Wild Weekend." This release was one of the first East Coast instrumentals with a surf feeling. A tight, aggressive electric guitar rocker from the Duane Eddy-/Link Wray instrumental school, "Wild Weekend" was a solid summer of 1962 hit and one of the first of many instrumentals serving as summer rock and roll anthems of the early and mid-60's.

Single Releases

As by The Rebels:

Marlee
    0094   "Wild Weekend"/"Wild Weekend Cha-Cha"   1962
           (also on Swan 4125)

As by The Rockin' Rebels:

Swan
    4140   "Rockin' Crickets"/"Hully Gully Rock"   1962

Dick Dale and The Del-Tones

Dick Dale and The Del-Tones was an expert, somewhat countrified, instrumental surf-rock group that produced the wild, drum-based instrumentals, "Let's Go Trippin" and "Miserlou" along with the deadpan vocal "Peppermint Man."

Single Releases

Deltone
    5012   "Oh Whee Marie"/"Breaking Heart"   1961
    5017   "Let's Go Trippin"/"Del-Tone Rock"
    5019   "Miserlou"/"Eight Till Midnight"
    5020   "Peppermint Man"/"Surf Beat"   1962

The Surfaris

The Surfaris had one excellent hit record, the droll "Surfer Joe" and the fine instrumental "Wipe Out."

Single Releases

Princess
—   "Wipe Out"/"Surfer Joe" (also on Dot 16479)   1963

The Righteous Brothers

The Righteous Brothers were an early duet with an effective rhythm and blues singing style that was so convincing that their early recordings were labeled "blue-eyed soul." Several of their Moonglow label releases were moderate hits. The energetically performed "Little Latin Lupe Lu," "My Babe" and "Ko Ko Joe" were done in much the same style as the hard-hitting Don and Dewey original (Specialty 639). Also taken from Don and Dewey was the equally effective shouter "Justine" (Specialty 631). Recording for the Philles label, The Righteous Brothers released the classic, "You've Lost That Lovin' Feeling," a best-seller featuring off-setting voices rendering marvelous lyrics. Some of their later single releases on the Verve label achieved best-seller success, but these releases were not as powerful because of their self-conscious lyrics and arrangements.

Single Releases

Moonglow
215	"Little Latin Lupe Lu"/"I'm So Lonely"	1963
223	"My Babe"/"Fee-Fi-Fidily-I-Oh"	
224	"Ko Ko Joe"/"B Flat Blues"	
231	"Try To Find Another Man"/"I Still Love You"	1964
234	"Bring Your Love To Me"/"If You're Lying, You'll Be Crying"	
235	"This Little Girl Of Mine"/"If You're Lying, You'll Be Crying"	
238	"Fannie Mae"/"Bring Your Love To Me"	

The Chambers Brothers

A first generation hard blues-rock group, The Chambers Brothers first recorded spirituals for the Proverb label and then blues for Vault with little commercial notice. The Chambers Brothers' style in these early Vault label recordings was earthy in nature and almost plodding in execution, but there were dynamic touches. The Chambers Brothers were early exponents of Los Angeles hard blues-rock. The twice-recorded "Time Has Come Today" and the two follow-up hits, "I Can't Stand It" and "All Strung Out Over You," each combined exciting vocals with energetic instrumental performances. The Chambers Brothers performed aggressive and occasionally dissonant rock and roll with heavy blues and gospel overtones.

Single Releases

Proverb
1021	"I Trust In God"/"Just A Little More Faith"	1963

Horizon
2	"Grizzly Bear"/"Gypsy Woman" (with Hoyt Axton)	1963

Vault
920	"Call Me"/"Seventeen"	1966
945	"Shout Pt. 1 & 2"	1968
955	"Just A Closer Walk With Thee"/"Girls We Love You"	1969
967	"House Of The Rising Sun"/"Blues Get Off My Shoulder"	

Columbia
43816	"Time Has Come Today"/"Dinah"	1966
43957	"All Strung Out Over You"/"Falling In Love"	1967
44080	"I Can't Stand It"/"Please Don't Leave Me"	
44296	"Uptown"/"Love Me Like The Rain"	
44414	"Time Has Come Today"/"People Get Ready"	1968
44679	"I Can't Turn You Loose"/"Do Your Thing"	
44779	"Are You Ready"/"You Got The Power To Turn Me On"	
44890	"Wake Up"	1969
44986	"My Baby Takes Care Of Business"/"Have A Little Faith"	
45055	"Merry Christmas Happy New Year"/"Did You Stop To Pray This Morning"	

NOTABLE LATIN ROCK GROUPS

Latin rock groups—Three Midniters, Cannibal and The Headhunters and The Village Callers—have been consistently popular in the Los Angeles area since 1965. Each of these groups has had a successful series of single releases, but the Latin rock sound, a gentle blend of rhythm and blues with jazz, only achieved national attention with The Santana rock group in 1969.

Thee Midniters

Thee Midniters were the most successful of the many East Los Angeles rhythm and blues vocal groups. Thee Midniters' hits, included the casually rendered classic oldie "Sad Girl," a full-tilt version of "Land Of 1000 Dances" and the cruisin' instrumental "Whittier Blvd."—named for a popular Los Angeles cruising locale.

Single Releases

Chattahoochee

666	"Land Of 1000 Dances"/"Ball O Twine"	1965
675	"Sad Girl"/"Heat Wave"	
684	"Whittier Blvd."/"Evil Love"	
693	"I Need Someone"/"Empty Heart"	
695	"Brother Where Are You"/"Heat Wave"	

Whittier

500	"Love Special Delivery"/"Don't Go Away"	1966
501	"It'll Never Be Over For Me"/"The Midnite Feeling"	
503	"Dragon Fly"/"The Big Ranch"	
504	"Never Knew I Had It So Bad"/"The Walking Song"	
507	"Jump Jive And Harmonize"/"Looking Out A Window"	1967

508   "Chile Con Soul"/"Tu Despedida"
509   "Breakfast On The Grass"/"Dreaming
        Casually"

Cannibal and The Headhunters

Cannibal and The Headhunters' recording of the natural dance-beat "Land Of 1000 Dances" was a minor Los Angeles area hit. Other good-sellers included the catchy upbeat "Nau Ninny Nau" and a James Brown original, "Out Of Sight."

Single Releases

Rampart
642   "Land Of 1000 Dances"/"I'll Show You How   1965
        To Love Me"
644   "Nau Ninny Nau"/"Here Comes Love"
646   "Follow The Music"/"I Need Your Loving"
654   "Out Of Sight"/"Please Baby Please"   1966

The Village Callers

The Village Callers were essentially a Latin jazz group. Their "Hector" was a minor rhythm and blues hit. They also recorded an excellent mid-tempo release of "Evil Ways," which later became the initial Santana hit.

Single Releases

Rampart
659   "Hector"/"I'm Leaving"   1968
683   "Evil Ways"/"When You're Gone"

Santana

Santana's solitary 60's hit was "Evil Ways." Santana continued their fine Latin rock sound into the 70's with "Black Magic Woman" (Columbia 45270) and "Oye Como Va" (Columbia 45330).

Single Release

Columbia
  45010   "Jingo"   1969
  45069   "Evil Ways"/"Waiting"

Creedence Clearwater Revival

This fine rock and roll group created a strange mixture of styles on their early single releases while searching for their own sound. As by Tommy Fogerty and The Blue Velvets, the group sang "Have You Ever Been Lonely" in the rocking style of Ritchie Valens and produced a sound similar to that of "La Bamba" (Del Fi 4110). Singles by The Golliwogs were also solid rock and roll, but the distinctive "Creedence" sound didn't emerge until the issue of "Porterville"—a medium rocker featuring a powerful Fogerty lead vocal with convincing lyrics. Even so, "Porterville" was only a minor hit, and it wasn't until the name change from The Golliwogs to Creedence Clearwater Revival and the release of "Susie Q"—a wild, powerful, extended version of the Dale Hawkins classic (Checker 863)—that the group really happened. Rendered with simplicity and force, subsequent releases were rooted deeply in the rhythm and blues and rockabilly music of the 50's. While almost everyone in San Francisco rock was becoming increasingly involved in psychedelia and hard rock gimmicks, Creedence maintained an honest-to-god, straightforward rock and roll style and continued to record excellent singles. The lyrics of the Southern-flavored "Proud Mary" and "Born On The Bayou"—inspiring the descriptive "swamp-rock" label—and especially of the ominous "Bad Moon Rising" were ideally suited to rock and roll. In fact, "Bad Moon Rising" is considered by some to be the best rock and roll record of the decade. Lyrics of the later "Fortunate Son" and "Who'll Stop The Rain" dealt with social issues, while such flip side recordings as the Little Richard style vocal "Travelin' Band" continued in the rock and roll groove.

Single Releases

As by Tommy Fogerty and The Blue Velvets:

Orchestra
1010	"Have You Ever Been Lonely"/"Bonita"	1961

As by The Golliwogs:

Fantasy
590	"Don't Tell Me No Lies"/"Little Girl Does Your Mama Know"	1964
597	"You Came Walking"/"Where You Been"	1965
599	"You Can't Be True"/"You Got Nothing On Me"	

Scorpio
404	"Brown Eyed Girl"/"You Better Be Careful"	1965
405	"Fight Fire"/"Fragile Child"	1966
408	"Walking On The Water"/"You Better Get It Before It Gets You"	1967
412	"Porterville"/"Call It Pretending"	

As by Creedence Clearwater Revival:

Fantasy
616	"Susie Q Pt. 1 & 2"	1968
617	"Walk On The Water"/"I Put A Spell On You"	

Sly and The Family Stone

Sylvester Stewart recorded one 50's style "do-wop" vocal group record for the G&P label, then rendered two mainly instrumental performances for San Francisco's Autumn label, all with negligible sales. His first Epic label release as by Sly with his group, The Family Stone, was the impressive hit "Dance To The Music," an intriguing combination of hard rock and exciting vocal group harmony. Later hits included "Everyday People," a statement of togetherness, the drug-oriented "I Want To Take You Higher" and "Hot Fun In The Summertime," a haltingly sung, rhythmic ballad featuring The Family Stone's intricate harmonies. Sly and The Family Stone sang about good times: good times getting high; good times dancing to the music.

Single Releases

As by Sylvester Stewart:

G&P

As by Sly:

Autumn

As by Sly and The Family Stone:

Loadstone

| 3951 | "I Ain't Got Nobody"/"I Can't Turn You Loose" | 1966 |

Epic

10256	"Dance To The Music"/"Let Me Hear It From You"	1967
10353	"M'Lady"/"Life"	1968
10407	"Everyday People"/"Sing A Simple Song"	
10450	"I Want To Take You Higher"/"Stand"	1969
10497	"Hot Fun In The Summertime"/"Fun"	
10555	"Everybody Is A Star"/"Thank You For Letting Me Be Myself Again"	

EARLY BRITISH ROCK AND ROLL

•

British pop music remained a world apart from American rock and roll during the late 50's and early 60's. American pop received heavy—if not selective—exposure on the British Isles, but the exchange was not mutual because British pop music was generally too conservative for the American rock and roll market. By the early 60's, many British mod rock and roll groups were developing a new pop form, frequently identified as "Mersey Beat." Many early releases by these groups used American rhythm and blues material. Most of these groups were obscure and remained obscure—Tony Knight and The Live Wires, Zoot Money and Farnon's Flamingos, among many, many others. Several British groups like The Graham Bond Organization and The Alex Korner Blues Inc. possessed considerable ability and served as spawning grounds for the personnel of later much better known British rock and roll groups. Those artists who emerged from the Mersey Beat base include The Quarrymen, known later as The Beatles; The Rolling Stones; The Alan Price Combo, without Price they became The Animals; The Kinks; and The Highnumbers, later known as The Who.

Scarcity and Value

Notwithstanding the fact that British label original-issue 45 RPM releases of these records are valuable, many

American label releases are of considerable collector interest. As this volume deals with collecting American label releases, these are the ones detailed in this section.

In dedication, perseverance and prices they are willing to meet towards amassing a complete body of Beatles material, Beatles collectors rival any other group of postwar record collectors, be they blues, 50's rhythm and blues or that very potent group of Elvis collectors. The complete Beatles library contains an incredible maze of trivia, including the Beatles "Flip Your Wig" parlor game, the early Beatles fan magazines and paperback books, recorded LP and 45 RPM interviews, the series of Christmas 45 RPM records spanning 1964–1969 which were available only to Beatles fan club members, bootlegged records by The Beatles and individual members (for instance, Ringo Starr's bootlegged 45 "I've Got A Woman"), the recorded works of early ex-Beatle Pete Best, along with all 45 RPM picture sleeves, and certainly not least, all original 45 RPM issues of all Beatles singles.

As with any other specialized collection, an entire Beatles record collection is worth much more than the cumulative value of the singles. The rarest American 45 RPM issues are the first two Vee Jay label singles and the second MGM single; each commands in excess of $10. The Atco issues, the other MGM and the German language Swan label single are valued in the $5 range, while the two later Vee Jay releases, the Tollie and the earliest Capitol singles bring from $2 to $5. The entire Capitol label 45 RPM series was recently reissued with identical Capitol release numbers on the Apple label. As they are no longer pressed, the Capitol label singles are now slightly more valuable.

Only singles by The Beatles and The Stones maintain constant value (though other early releases by The Who, Joe Cocker on Phillips, Rod Stewart on Press, Manfred Mann on Prestige along with both early and late obscure Kinks and Yardbirds single releases can bring over $2). The briefly available single "Stoned" by The Rolling Stones can bring around $20. The next five Rolling Stones

45 RPM issues are valued in the $2 range, while later singles are in less demand. Depending mainly on an unstable demand, values will certainly gell as issues become scarce.

The Beatles

The Beatles revitalized American rock and roll and led to the success of the British Mersey Beat sound, which was performed by over one hundred British groups and single artists of varying styles and abilities.

The earliest American single releases of Beatles material were simultaneously issued on at least six labels. Vee Jay records jumped the competition with the 1963 release of two singles, "Please Please Me" and "From Me To You," but both releases were withdrawn by year's end because of poor sales. In 1964, Capitol issued "I Want To Hold Your Hand," an instant best-seller. Immediately both Atco and MGM released some very early Beatles singles that were artistically less than satisfying performances. Singles on the Swan and Vee Jay labels were more representative of the then current Beatles style and thus became much better sellers. However, by this time, Capitol had already secured exclusive rights to all post-1964 Beatles releases.

The Beatles were an excellent barometer of musical tastes throughout the 60's. Their early singles were drab imitations of American blues artists, as with Jimmy Reed's "Take Out Some Insurance" (Vee Jay 314). Another first generation British group, The Rolling Stones, was more effective with this blues style.

The first hits by The Beatles were rendered in a light-hearted pop-flavored style. While several other British groups, especially The Zombies, were successful with several well-designed pop hits, The Beatles proved considerably more durable than their competition. The difference was that The Beatles were able to abandon one sound, such as blues, and successfully adapt to new forms, while many other British groups were unable to progress greatly from their earliest styles.

The Beatles continued to improve upon their original pop sound while simultaneously innovating new approaches to their music. During 1964–1965, The Beatles recorded rock and roll almost exclusively, with a few ballads appearing on Capitol label singles. Their delicate ballad, "Yesterday," released in 1965, became the best selling non-rock and roll hit of the year. While recording better and better ballads, in particular the wistful "Eleanor Rigby" and the powerful "Hey Jude," The Beatles progressed into even better rock and roll with "Lady Madonna," "Get Back" and "The Ballad Of John And Yoko"—three of the outstanding rock and roll records of the 60's.

Single Releases

Vee Jay

498	"Please Please Me"/"Ask Me Why"	1963
522	"From Me To You"/"Thank You Girl"	
581	"From Me To You"/"Please Please Me"	1964
	(also on Capitol 6063)	
587	"Do You Want To Know A Secret"/"Thank You Girl" (also on Capitol 6064)	

Swan

4152	"She Loves You"/"I'll Get You"	1963
4182	"Sie Liebt Dich"/"I'll Get You"	1964

Tollie

9001	"Twist And Shout"/"There's A Place"	1964
	(also on Capitol 6061)	
9008	"P.S. I Love You"/"Love Me Do"	
	(also on Capitol 6062)	

Atco

6302	"Sweet Georgia Brown"/"Take Out Some Insurance On Me Baby"	1964
6308	"Ain't She Sweet"/"Nobody's Child"	

MGM

| 13213 | "My Bonnie"/"When The Saints" | 1964 |
| 13227 | "Why"/"Cry For A Shadow" | |

Capitol

5112	"I Want To Hold Your Hand"/"I Saw Her Standing There"	1964
5150	"Can't Buy Me Love"/"You Can't Do That"	
6065	"Roll Over Beethoven"/"Misery"	
6066	"All My Loving"/"This Boy"	
5222	"A Hard Day's Night"/"I Should Have Known Better"	
5234	"I'll Cry Instead"/"I'm Happy Just To Dance With You"	
5235	"And I Love Her"/"If I Fell"	
5255	"Slow Down"/"Matchbox"	
5327	"I Feel Fine"/"She's A Woman"	
5371	"Eight Days A Week"/"I Don't Want To Spoil The Party"	1965
5407	"Ticket To Ride"/"Yes It Is"	
5476	"I'm Down"/"Help"	
5498	"Yesterday"/"Act Naturally"	
5555	"Day Tripper"/"We Can Work It Out"	
5587	"Nowhere Man"/"What Goes On"	1966
5651	"Paperback Writer"/"Rain"	
5715	"Yellow Submarine"/"Eleanor Rigby"	
5810	"Penny Lane"/"Strawberry Fields Forever"	
5964	"All You Need Is Love"/"Baby You're A Rich Man"	1967
2056	"Hello Goodbye"/"I Am The Walrus"	
2138	"Lady Madonna"/"The Inner Light"	1968

Apple

2276	"Hey Jude"/"Revolution"	1968
2490	"Get Back"/"Don't Let Me Down"	1969
2531	"The Ballad Of John And Yoko"/"Old Brown Shoe"	
2654	"Come Together"/"Something"	

As by The Plastic Ono Band:

Apple
  1809 "Give Peace A Chance"/"Remember Love"   1969
  1813 "Cold Turkey"/"Don't Worry Kyoko"

The Rolling Stones

The Rolling Stones are an exceptional British blues-rock group. "Stoned," their initial U.S. release, was withdrawn because of the drug implications of the title even though the record was an instrumental with no overt references to narcotics. "Not Fade Away" and "It's All Over Now" were thumping, vigorous rock and roll releases, while "Time Is On My Side" and "Heart Of Stone" were tight, rolling blues ballads.

"Satisfaction" was the Stones' first major break with the basic blues mold. By becoming the major rock and roll hit of 1965, "Satisfaction" established The Rolling Stones as the definitive British rock and roll group, and from then on, most releases by The Rolling Stones were aggressive rock and roll, such as the powerfully exciting "Jumpin' Jack Flash" and the rebelliously menacing "Street Fighting Man." Interspersed among these rockers were such ballad releases as "Lady Jane" and "Ruby Tuesday"—the latter became a best-seller only because the flip, "Let's Spend The Night Together" was banned from top-40 radio. Other ballads, such as "Dandelion" and "The Lantern" represented a relatively weak "flower power" phase for The Rolling Stones. Undeniably, The Rolling Stones were at their best with their specialty—powerful rock and roll.

Single Releases

London
  9641 "Stoned"/"I Wanna Be Your Man"   1964

9657	"Not Fade Away"/"I Wanna Be Your Man"	
9682	"I Just Want To Make Love To You"/"Tell Me"	
9687	"It's All Over Now"/"Good Times Bad Times"	
9708	"Time Is On My Side"/"Congratulations"	
9725	"Heart Of Stone"/"What A Shame"	1965
9741	"The Last Time"/"Play With Fire"	
9766	"Satisfaction"/"Under Assistant West Coast Promotion Man"	
9792	"Get Off My Cloud"/"I'm Free"	
9808	"As Tears Go By"/"Gotta Get Away"	
9823	"19th Nervous Breakdown"/"Sad Day"	1966
901	"Paint It Black"/"Stupid Girl"	
902	"Mother's Little Helper"/"Lady Jane"	
903	"Have You Ever Seen Your Mother, Baby, Standing In The Shadow"/"Who's Driving My Plane"	
904	"Ruby Tuesday"/"Let's Spend The Night Together"	1967
905	"Dandelion"/"We Love You"	
906	"She's A Rainbow"/"Two Thousand Light Years From Home"	
907	"The Lantern"/"In Another Land" (by Bill Wyman)	
908	"Jumpin' Jack Flash"/"Child Of The Moon"	1968
909	"Street Fighting Man"/"No Expectations"	
910	"Honky Tonk Woman"/"You Can't Always Get What You Want"	1969

As by Marianne Faithful:

London
| 1022 | "Sister Morphine"/"Something Better" | 1969 |

The Animals

The earliest single releases by The Animals were largely adaptations of blues-and-folk based songs. They recorded Bob Dylan's "Baby Let Me Follow You Down"—a variation of the earlier blues standard "Baby Don't You Tear My Clothes"—as the retitled "Baby Let Me Take You Home." The Animals' first major hit was the folk song "House Of The Rising Sun." Their later successes included the John Lee Hooker original (Vee Jay 438) "Boom Boom" and the blues classic "See See Rider"—each done in the somber, frequently gloomy style of lead singer, Eric Burdon. Though Burdon attempted to infuse power into his vocals, most of The Animals' recordings were neither dynamic nor compelling. Perhaps this was because of the groups' repetitively downbeat approach to such overly serious original material as "We've Gotta Get Out Of This Place" and "It's My Life." In the latter part of the 60's, The Animals dwelt upon compositions dealing with the psychedelic "flower power" movement, as in "San Franciscan Nights" and "Monterey."

Single Releases

MGM

13242	"Baby Let Me Take You Home"/"Gonna Send You Back To Walker"	1964
13264	"House Of The Rising Sun"/"Talking Bout You"	
13273	"I'm Crying"/"Take It Easy Baby"	
13298	"Boom Boom"/"Blue Feeling"	
13311	"Don't Let Me Be Misunderstood"/"Club A Go Go"	1965
13339	"Bring It On Home"/"For Miss Caulker"	
13389	"We've Gotta Get Out Of This Place"/"I Can't Believe It"	
13414	"It's My Life"/"I'm Going To Change The World"	
13468	"Inside Looking Out"/"You're On My Mind"	1966
13514	"Don't Bring Me Down"/"Cheating"	
13582	"See See Rider"/"She'll Return It"	
13636	"Help Me Girl"/"That Ain't Where It's At"	
13721	"San Franciscan Nights"/"Good Times"	1967

13791   "When I Was Young"/"A Girl Named Sandoz"
13868   "Monterey"/"Ain't That So"
13917   "Anything"/"It's All Meat"   1968
13939   'Sky Pilot Pt. 1 & 2"
14013   "White Horses"/"River Deep—Mountain
        High"

The Kinks

The first few recordings by The Kinks were unpolished straight-out rock and roll performances. In particular, the off-key "You Really Got Me" and "Who'll Be The Next In Line" were brash and discordant songs with barren yet appealing lyrics. Some early releases by The Kinks were patterned after the styles of Little Richard and Bo Diddley. Subsequent single releases, such as "A Well Respected Man" and "Dedicated Followers Of Fashion," were satirical put-downs of the straight world. Despite their easy target, these records were effective and quite popular. Though their mid-60's releases sold well, the popularity of The Kinks declined in 1967, and several singles from this period—such as "Death Of A Clown" and "Days" —are now quite scarce. In the late 60's and early 70's, The Kinks rediscovered success. Their fine 1970 release of "Lola" (Reprise 0930) is a quite lovely song with sympathetic references to transvestism—a far cry from the wild, early Kinks.

Single Releases

Cameo
  308   "Long Tall Sally"/"I Took My Baby Home"   1964
        (also on Cameo 345)
  348   "You Still Want Me"/"You Do Something To
        Me"

Reprise
  0306 "You Really Got Me"/"It's All Right"   1964

Manfred Mann

Manfred Mann was at first a rock and roll unit with a distinct Chicago blues feel. The Prestige label release "5-4-3-2-1" is a very bluesy performance skillfully drawn from Bo Diddley and Muddy Waters influences. "Do Wah Diddy Diddy" is a successful rock and roll performance with few traces of the early blues approach. Manfred Mann achieved major hit status with two Bob Dylan compositions, "Just Like A Woman" and the top-10 smash, the well-executed "The Mighty Quinn." By the late 60's, Manfred Mann had become more subdued, both in performance and material, as is apparent in the humorous "My Name Is Jack" which little resembles the early 60's Manfred Mann blues group.

Single Releases

Prestige

312	"5-4-3-2-1"/"Without You"	1964

Ascot

2157	"Do Wah Diddy Diddy"/"What You Gonna Do"	1964
2165	"Sha La La"/"John Hardy"	1965
2170	"Come Tomorrow"/"What Did I Do Wrong"	
2194	"If You Gotta Go, Go Now"/"The One In The Middle"	
2210	"She Needs Company"/"Hi Lili Hi Lo"	1966

United Artists

55040	"Pretty Flamingo"/"You're Standing By"	1966
55066	"When Will I Be Loved"/"Do You Have To Do That"	

Mercury

72607	"Just Like A Woman"/"I Wanna Be Rich"	1966
72629	"Semi-Detached Suburban Mr. James"/"Each And Every Day"	
72675	"Ha Ha Said The Clown"/"Feeling So Good"	1967
72770	"The Mighty Quinn"/"By Request Edwin Garvey"	
72822	"My Name Is Jack"/"There Is A Man"	1968
72879	"Fox On The Run"/"Too Many People"	
72921	"Ragamuffin Man"/"A B Side"	1969

Polydor

14097	"Please Mrs. Henry"/"Prayer"	1969

The Who

The Who recorded some great, dominant back-beat rock and roll complete with fascinating, often disdainful lyrics. Just as Chuck Berry in his "School Days" (Chess 1653) and Eddie Cochran in his "Summertime Blues" (Liberty 55144) captured and distilled the spirit of 50's teenage life, The Who made the same statements for the kids of the 60's in "My Generation," "The Kids Are Alright" and "I'm A Boy." The Who embellished Cochran's "Summertime Blues" with hard rock devices and turned this 50's teenage anthem into a major 60's hit. The Who not only performed exquisite rock and roll, they also added sardonic bite to such original compositions as "I Can See For Miles," "Substitute" and "Pinball Wizard"— all flirtatious expressions of wisdom.

Single Releases

Decca
31725	"I Can't Explain"/"Bald Headed Woman"	1965
31801	"Anyway, Anyhow, Anywhere"/"Anytime You Want Me"	
31877	"My Generation"/"Out In The Street"	1966
31988	"The Kids Are Alright"/"A Legal Matter"	
32058	"I'm A Boy"/"In The City"	
32114	"Happy Jack"/"Whiskey Man"	1967
32156	"Pictures Of Lily"/"Doctor Doctor"	
32206	"I Can See For Miles"/"Mary-Anne With The Shakey Hands"	
32288	"Call Me Lightning"/"Dr. Jekyll And Mr. Hyde"	1968
32362	"Magic Bus"/"Someone's Coming"	
32465	"Pinball Wizard"/"Dogs Pt. 2"	
32519	"I'm Free'/"We're Not Gonna Take It"	1969
32670	"The Seeker"/"Here For More"	
32708	"Summertime Blues"/"Heaven And Hell"	

Atco

   6509   "Substitute"/"Waltz For A Pig"   1966

Them

Originally from Ireland, Them recorded the major hit "Gloria" which was released twice on the American Parrot label. "Gloria" featured lead singer Van Morrison performing in an unusually vital and confident manner with exceptional up-tempo instrumental support. "Gloria," "Here Comes The Night"—a fine blues ballad—and the transfixing "Mystic Eyes" were among the best of very early British rock and roll.

Single Releases

Parrot

356	"Gloria"/"If You And I Could Be As Two"	1965
9727	"Gloria"/"Baby Please Don't Go"	
9749	"Here Comes The Night"/"All For Myself"	
9784	"Gonna Dress In Black"/"It Won't Hurt"	
9796	"Mystic Eyes"/"If You And I Could Be As Two"	
9819	"Call My Name"/"Bring Em On In"	1966
3003	"Don't You Know"/"Richard Cory"	
3006	"I Can Only Give You Everything"/"Don't Start Crying Now"	

The Yardbirds

The Yardbirds were a major first generation British rock and roll group with a sound that is best described as "pop-blues." The Yardbirds' first hit single was the engaging "For Your Love," which featured the guitar work of Eric Clapton behind a rather controlled lead vocal style. "Heart Full Of Soul" is a moderately sung rocker while

"Still I'm Sad" possesses a hypnotic chanting beat with perfectly matched guitar work—again both were major hits. The introspective "Shapes Of Things" and the varied-tempo "Over Under Sideways Down" were also successful releases. The Yardbirds went into a decline after 1967 with the emergence of a harder British rock sound. Ironically, this "heavy" school of rock was championed by Eric Clapton, this time around with Cream. The Yardbirds adopted a more powerful instrumental approach with the release of "Happenings Ten Years Time Ago" and "Little Games," but the vocals continued to be almost inappropriately mild in contrast to the hard rock sound.

Single Releases

Epic

9709	"I Wish You Would"/"I Ain't Got You"	1965
9709	"I Wish You Would"/"A Certain Girl"	
9790	"For Your Love"/"Got To Hurry"	
9823	"Heart Full Of Soul"/"Steeled Blues"	
9857	"Still I'm Sad"/"I'm A Man"	
9891	"Shapes Of Things"/"I'm Not Talking"	1966
10006	"Shapes Of Things"/"New York City Blues"	
10035	"Over Under Sideways Down"/"Jeff's Boogie"	
10094	"Happenings Ten Years Time Ago"/"The Nazz Are Blue"	
10156	"Little Games"/"Puzzles"	1967
10204	"Ha Ha Said The Clown"/"Tinker Tailor Soldier Sailor"	
10248	"Ten Little Indians"/"Drinking Muddy Water"	
10303	"Goodnight Sweet Josephine"/"Think About It"	1968

Joe Cocker

Joe Cocker's recording career began with his little-noted rendition of the Lennon-McCartney composition "I'll Cry

Instead." A rough-edged shouter, Cocker's vocal quality is best described as that of an English Ray Charles. His first hit was with another Lennon-McCartney song, the intensely performed "With A Little Help From My Friends." Assisted by the wild pounding piano work of Leon Russell, Cocker's follow-up hits included the frantic "Feelin' Alright," Leon Russell's sensuous "Delta Lady" and a third Lennon-McCartney original, "She Came In The Bathroom Window." Another fine Cocker effort was the tireless, nonstop version of the standard "Cry Me A River." Joe Cocker was a genuinely exciting 60's rock and roll singer who combined great vocal energy with uncompromising rock and roll arrangements.

Single Releases

Philips

40255	"I'll Cry Instead"/"Precious Words"	1965

A&M

928	"Marjorine"/"New Age Of The Lily"	1967
991	"With A Little Help From My Friends"/"Bye Bye Blackbird"	1968
1083	"Feeling Alright"/"Sandpaper Cadillac"	
1112	"Delta Lady"/"She's So Good To Me"	
1147	"She Came In The Bathroom Window"/ "Change In Louise"	1969
1174	"The Letter"/"Space Captain"	
1200	"Cry Me A River"/"Give Peace A Chance"	

Van Morrison

After his 1967 parting from Them, Van Morrison's first American single release was the knees-up, good-time rock and roll hit "Brown Eyed Girl." Morrison's releases on the Warner Brothers label included the warmly produced ballad "Crazy Love," the intriguing upbeat "Domino" and fast-talking, rhythmic "Blue Money." All are fine examples of pop rock and roll not taking itself at all seriously, just meant for a good time. This extra dimension makes the talented Van Morrison especially effective. All of his recordings, both with Them and as a single, are good fun to listen to.

Single Releases

Bang
545	"Brown Eyed Girl"/"Goodbye Baby"	1967
552	"Chick A Boom"/"Ro Ro Rosey"	

Warner Brothers
7383	"Crazy Love"/"Come Running"	1968
7434	"Domino"/"Sweet Jannie"	
7462	"Blue Money"/"Sweet Thing"	1969
7488	"Street Choir"/"Call Me Up In Dreamland"	
7543	"Tupelo Honey"/"Starting A New Life"	

NOTABLE BRITISH ROCK AND ROLL ARTISTS

The Zombies

The Zombies had two early hits, the relaxed pop-styled "She's Not There" and "Tell Her No." The 1967 release "Time Of The Season" was also a hit and has since become a rock classic. In the era of the harsher British blues groups, the style of The Zombies remained rather tame.

Single Releases

Parrot
9695	"She's Not There"/"You Make Me Feel So Good"	1964
9723	"Tell Her No"/"Leave Me Be"	1965
9747	"She's Coming Home"/"I Must Move"	

9769	"I Want You Back Again"/"Remember When I Loved Her"	
9786	"I Love You"/"Whenever You Are Ready"	
9797	"Just Out Of Reach"/"Remember You"	
9821	"Don't Go Away"/"Is This The Dream"	1966
3004	"Indication"/"How We Were Before"	

Date

1604	"Time Of The Season"/"I'll Call You Mine"	1967
1612	"This Will Be Our Year"/"Butcher's Tail"	
1628	"Time Of The Season"/"Friends Of Mine"	1968
1644	"Imagine The Swan"/"Conversation Of Floral Street"	1969
1648	"Don't Cry For Me"/"If It Don't Work Out"	

The Spencer Davis Group

The Spencer Davis Group specialized in danceable rhythm and blues with the high-speed "Keep On Running" and "Gimme Some Loving." As with early releases by The Righteous Brothers, The Davis Group achieved a fine rhythm and blues sound that received air play on otherwise all black rhythm and blues radio stations.

Single Releases

Atco

6400	"Keep On Running"/"High Time Baby"	1966
6416	"Somebody Help Me"/"Stevie's Blues"	

United Artists

50108	"Gimme Some Loving"/"Blues In F"	1967
50144	"I'm A Man"/"I Can't Get Enough Of It"	
50162	"Somebody Help Me"/"On The Green Light"	
50202	"Time Seller"/"I Don't Want You No More"	
50286	"Looking Back"/"After Tea"	1968

Rod Stewart

Rod Stewart, originally with Python Lee Johnson, recorded the fast-tempo blues classic "Good Morning Little Schoolgirl," but received little notice. In 1971, Stewart's career rocketed with the blistering "Maggie May" (Mercury 73224), a major smash hit.

Single Releases

As by Python Lee Johnson:

GNP
    449   "In A Broken Dream"/"Doin' Fine"   1966

As by Rod Stewart:

Press
   9722   "Good Morning Little Schoolgirl"/"I'm Gonna   1967
           Move To The Outskirts Of Town"

SAN FRANCISCO ROCK

•

The emergence of The Jefferson Airplane drew attention to "hard rock" and to a good number of San Francisco rock groups. In turn, this hard rock sound had an enormous impact on later American and British rock music. Until the San Francisco rock thrust, American rock and roll music was in the doldrums; the focus was on soul music—mostly Memphis and Motown—and on British pop. San Francisco rock groups rekindled American rock and roll, and in the bargain, rock music was born.

Rock is not rock and roll—which is classically a fusion of rhythm and blues with country-music derived rockabilly. Rather this was "rock," furious vocal performances mixed with shattering instrumental work to present an enormous recorded impact. Intense amplification was the key to rock. Often embellished with distortion and feedback, this amplification strongly suggested disoriented violence. Though an extension of rock and roll, blues and other ingredients, rock was just as clearly a separate musical form that broadly influenced the whole spectrum of pop music. These influences are apparent in the emergence of Cream and Jimi Hendrix on the British scene and in the new approaches of established rhythm and blues artists such as The Temptations, Stevie Wonder and Ike and Tina Turner.

Besides the emphasis on electronic amplification as an integral part of instrumentation, another element unique to hard rock was the importance that drugs played in communicating the overall message. Several important songs, including The Jefferson Airplane's "White Rabbit," and Sly and The Family Stone's "I Want To Take You Higher," conveyed an unmistakable drug statement. Apart from the blunt lyrics, such effects as fuzz and feedback distortion were used, most notably by Jimi Hendrix, to produce the effects of a drug-induced experience.

Towards the decade's end, this "heavy" approach to rock became a bit contrived and self-conscious. With the diminishment of the underground movement, drug advocacy lost some of its clout, and thus hard rock lost some gloss. It was partly in response to the psychedelic power play of the late 60's that a simpler turn to the less pretentious music of the 50's gained a strong 70's foothold.

The Jefferson Airplane

The Jefferson Airplane was a formative group of early San Francisco hard rock. The throbbing vocals were provided by the explosive Gracie Slick of the Great Society—Gracie Slick replaced Signe Anderson, who appears on the first several singles. The Airplane first hit with the bold rocker "Somebody To Love" and the climax-building "White Rabbit." For the most part, The Jefferson Airplane recorded turbulent, professional rock with wry, provocative lyrics. Occasionally they featured drug-related compositions, such as the hit "White Rabbit," an analogy between hallucinogens and Alice's experience in Wonderland.

Single Releases

RCA
8769   "It's No Secret"/"Runnin' Around This World"   1966
8848   "Come Up The Years"/"Blues From An
           Airplane"

8967	"Bringing Me Down"/"Let Me In"	
9063	"My Best Friend"/"How Do You Feel"	
9140	"Somebody To Love"/"She Has Funny Cars"	1967
9248	"White Rabbit"/"Plastic Fantastic Lover"	
9297	"Ballad Of You And Me And Pooneil"/"Two Heads"	
9389	"Watch Her Ride"/"Martha"	
9496	"Greasy Heart"/"Share A Little Joke"	1968
9644	"Crown Of Creation"/"Lather"	
0245	"Volunteers"/"We Can Be Together"	1969
0150	"Plastic Fantastic Lover"/"Other Side Of This Life"	

As by Gracie Slick and The Great Society:

Columbia

44583	"Sally Go Round The Roses"	1968

Big Brother and The Holding Company

Big Brother and The Holding Company featured the harsh, blustery blues vocals of the late Janis Joplin. The Mainstream label releases were little-noted, esoteric records. Several of these recordings—especially "Down On Me"—were unusually poor, muddily recorded transcriptions, but the raw, intense Joplin style largely overwhelmed these deficiencies of production. Janis Joplin exploded on the rock scene with the mighty Columbia label release "Piece Of My Heart." She soon outshone The Holding Company and left them before the end of the decade.

Single Releases

Mainstream

657	"All Is Loneliness"/"Blindman"	1967
662	"Down On Me"/"Call On Me"	

666 "Bye Bye Baby"/"Intruder"
675 "Women Is Losers"/"Caterpillar"   1968
678 "Coo Coo"/"The Last Time"

Columbia
44626 "Piece Of My Heart"/"Turtle Blues"   1969
45023 "Kozmic Blues"/"One Good Man" (with the
        Kozmic Blues Band)

LOS ANGELES ROCK
•

The earliest second generation Los Angeles rock group was the tasty and professional Buffalo Springfield. Later Los Angeles rock groups, especially the forceful Doors and Steppenwolf and the blues-based Canned Heat, specialized in a much harder rock sound.

The Buffalo Springfield

The Buffalo Springfield was an important post-60's rock unit. Their early releases, particularly the hit "For What It's Worth," contained effective social impact. "For What It's Worth" is a low-keyed, biting narrative about the Sunset Strip riots. The Springfield performed lyrically brilliant rock and roll with the crisp "Bluebird" and "Mr. Soul." After a series of excellent Atco label single releases, The Buffalo Springfield disbanded into several rock and folk rock groups. The most celebrated of these groups was the immensly popular Crosby, Stills and Nash—David Crosby of The Byrds; Stephen Stills, composer of "For What It's Worth" and "Bluebird"; and Graham Nash. Shortly thereafter, Neil Young, another ex-Springfield member, joined the group. The Buffalo Springfield produced a number of fine, developing rock talents and provided an early vehicle for several of the major rock stars of the 70's.

Single Releases

As by The Buffalo Springfield:

Atco

6428	"Nowadays Clancy Can't Even Sing"/"Go And Say Goodbye"	1966
6452	"Burned"/"Everybody's Wrong"	
6459	"For What It's Worth"/"Do I Have To Come Right Out And Say It"	1967
6499	"Bluebird"/"Mr. Soul"	
6519	"Rock N Roll Woman"/"A Child's Claim To Fame"	
6545	"Expecting To Fly"/"Everydays"	
6572	"Uno-Mundo"/"Merry-Go-Round"	1968
6602	"Kind Woman"/"Special Care"	
6615	"On The Way Home"/Four Days Gone"	

As by Crosby, Stills and Nash:

Atlantic

2652	"Marrakesh Express"/"Hopelessly Hoping"	1969
2676	"Suite: Judy Blue Eyes"/"Long Time Gone"	

The Doors

Featuring the intense brooding voice of the late Jim Morrison, The Doors recorded the enormously successful blockbuster hit single of 1967, "Light My Fire." "Light My Fire," a hypnotically sexual performance by Morrison, gave The Doors a reputation for recording lyrics with strong erotic overtones, but The Doors also sing rock with wit and power. "People Are Strange" is a sympathetic portrayal of nonconformity; "The Unknown Soldier" is an indignant proclamation of war's end. Performances by The

Doors generally have a dark edge and are slightly sinister in execution.

Single Releases

Elektra

45611	"End Of The Night"/"Break On Through"	1967
45615	"Light My Fire"/"The Crystal Ship"	
45621	"People Are Strange"/"Unhappy Girl"	
45624	"Love Me Two Times"/"Moonlight Drive"	
45628	"The Unknown Soldier"/"We Could Be So Good Together"	1968
45635	"Hello I Love You, Won't You Tell Me Your Name"/"Love Street"	
45646	"Touch Me"/"Wild Child"	
45656	"Wishful Sinful"/"Who Scared You"	1969
45663	"Tell All The People"/"Easy Ride"	
45673	"Runnin' Blue"/"Do It"	

Steppenwolf

Steppenwolf, originally The Sparrow, combined literate lyrics with brutally forceful rock to create their two stone hits, "Born To Be Wild" and the whirlwind rocker "Magic Carpet Ride." Subsequent releases were of comparable quality but achieved only moderate hit status.

Single Releases

Immediate

502	"Telephone Blues"	1967

As by The Sparrow:

Columbia

43755	"Isn't It Strange"/"Tomorrow's Ship"	1966
43960	"Green Bottle Lover"/"Down Goes Your Love Life"	1967

As by Steppenwolf:

Dunhill

4109	"The Ostrich"/"A Girl I Knew"	1968
4138	"Born To Be Wild"/"Everybody's Next One"	
4160	"Magic Carpet Ride"/"Sookie Sookie"	
4182	"Rock Me"/"Jupiter Child"	1969
4192	"It's Never Too Late"/"Happy Birthday"	
4205	"Move Over"/"Power Play"	
4221	"Monster"/"Berry Rides Again"	

Canned Heat

Possessing a hard-rock blues sound, Canned Heat adapted authentic blues material—such as "Rollin' And Tumblin," from Muddy Waters (Aristocrat 412) and "One Kind Favor," a Lightning Hopkins song (RPM 359)—to a hard rock performance. Several compositions unique to Canned Heat, especially the good-natured "Boogie Music," neatly captured a blues mood. Canned Heat had two 1968 back-to-back hits, both featuring the hypnotically detached, high-pitched voice of the late Al "Nite Owl" Wilson—the high-speed "On The Road Again" and "Going Up The Country." Strangely, Canned Heat, a most professional rock band and self-acknowledged blues band, often lacked an essential blues element—the emotional performance. "Sic 'Em Pigs" was a moderate hit with provocative lyrics—the "pigs" are members of the Los Angeles County Sheriff's Department—and a none too subtle approach. In 1969, Canned Heat had another best-seller with "Let's Work Together," a Wilbert Harrison original (Fury 1059), this time featuring a hard-hitting instrumental and vocal approach.

Single Releases

Liberty

55979	"Rollin' And Tumblin' "/"Bullfrog Blues"	1967

56038	"On The Road Again"/"Boogie Music"	1968
56077	"Going Up The Country"/"One Kind Favor"	
56079	"Christmas Blues"/"The Chipmunk Song" (with The Chipmunks)	
56097	"Time Was"/"Low Down"	1969
56127	"Sic 'Em Pigs"/"Poor Moon"	
56151	"Let's Work Together"/"I'm Her Man"	
56180	"Going Up The Country"/"Future Blues"	

BRITISH HARD ROCK

•

An amalgam of hard rock with a British blues feel, British hard rock was best portrayed by the stunning work of Cream and through the strong feedback-induced psychedelic effects of Jimi Hendrix. By this time, the pop Mersey Beat had given way to rock, and many of the softer British groups had long since faded. Established British groups, especially The Beatles and The Who, put a harder rock edge on their post-1967 work.

Cream

An important second-wave British rock group, Cream was the self-proclaimed best of British rock talent. Eric Clapton (of the earlier Yardbirds) provided lead guitar and vocals and gave the recorded sound of Cream a grainy-textured quality. That Cream drew heavily upon blues material for their early single releases is especially evident in their extended version of the Chicago blues original by Howlin' Wolf, "Spoonful" (Chess 1762). "Sunshine Of Your Love," a slow-breaking song that eventually became a major hit, united riveting guitar work with a direct, on-target vocal. "White Room" was a bigger hit single that used similar instrumental work with forceful drug-inspired lyrics. Essentially, Cream was the epitome of the "heavy"

217

British rock group sound; the group combined transfixing lyrics with an explosive instrumental impact.

Single Releases

Atco
6462	"I Feel Fine"/"N.S.U."	1967
6488	"Strange Brew"/"Tales Of Brave Ulysses"	
6522	"Spoonful Pt. 1 & 2"	
6544	"Sunshine Of Your Love"/"Swlabr"	
6575	"Pressed Rat And Warthog"/"Anyone For Tennis"	1968
6617	"White Room"/"Those Were The Days"	
6646	"Crossroads"/"Passing The Time"	
6668	"What A Bringdown"/"Badge"	1969
6708	"Lawdy Mama"/"Sweet Wine"	

The Jimi Hendrix Experience

Jimi Hendrix was an American-born musician with early 60's rhythm and blues session experience. Hendrix exploded onto the British rock scene with his 1967 single release "Hey Joe," a restrained blues vocal with stormy guitar work. The Jimi Hendrix Experience sound then progressed into more turbulent recordings with "Foxey Lady" and Bob Dylan's "All Along The Watchtower." Hendrix's most controversial work was the 1970 hard rock version of "The Star-Spangled Banner" (Reprise 1044). The late Jimi Hendrix's contribution to British rock was that of fire-breathing anarchy, a sort of self-consuming rock intensity.

Single Releases

As by Jimi Hendrix:

Audio Fidelity
167	"No Such Animal Pt. 1 & 2" (with Curtis Knight)	1967

As by The Jimi Hendrix Experience:

Reprise

0572	"Hey Joe"/"51st Anniversary"	1967
0597	"Purple Haze"/"The Wind Cries Mary"	
0641	"Foxey Lady"/"Hey Joe"	
0665	"Up From The Skies"/"One Rainy Wish"	1968
0728	"Foxey Lady"/"Purple Haze"	
0767	"All Along The Watchtower"/"Burning Of The Midnight Lamp"	1969
0792	"Crosstown Traffic"/"Gypsy Eyes"	
0853	"Stone Free"/"If Six Was Nine"	

NOTABLE BRITISH HARD ROCK GROUPS

The Small Faces

The Small Faces produced a good-time, hard rock sound complete with psychedelic, drug-oriented overtones in the hit, "Itchycoo Park," an adventure in getting high.

Single Releases

Press

9826	"Sha-La-La-La-Lee"/"Grow Your Own"	1966
5007	"Hey Girl"/"Almost Grown"	

RCA

8949	"All Or Nothing"/"Understanding"	1966
9055	"My Mind's Eye"/"I Can't Dance With You"	

Immediate

501	"Itchycoo Park"/"I'm Only Dreaming"	1967
5003	"Tin Soldier"/"I Feel Much Better"	1968
5007	"Lazy Sunday"/"Rolling Over"	
5009	"Donkey Rides And Penny A Glass"/"Universal"	
5012	"Mad John"/"The Journey"	1969

5014   "Afterglow Of Your Love"/"Wham Bam, Thank You Mam"

John Mayall's Bluesbreakers

John Mayall's Bluesbreakers, featuring the post-Yardbirds, pre-Cream Eric Clapton, was an extraordinary slow blues group that performed largely traditional compositions.

Single Releases

Immediate
| 502 | "Telephone Blues" | 1967 |

London
20016	"Parchman Farm"/"Key To Love"	1967
20035	"Oh Pretty Woman"/"Suspicious"	
20037	"Picture On The Wall"/"Jenny"	
20042	"Walking On Sunset"/"Living Alone"	1968

Polydor
| 14004 | "Don't Waste My Time"/"Don't Pick A Flower" | 1969 |

Procol Harum

Procol Harum had initial success with the mystical somber tones of their good-sized off-beat hit, "A Whiter Shade Of Pale." They had less success with similarly styled A&M label releases.

Single Releases

Deram
| 7507 | "A Whiter Shade Of Pale"/"Lime Street Blues" | 1967 |

A&M
| 885 | "Homburg"/"Good Captain Clack" | 1967 |

927 "Quite Rightly So"/"In The Wee Small Hours
     Of Sixpence"   1968
1069 "A Salty Dog"/"Long Gone Geek"
1111 "Devil Came From Kansas"/"Boredom"

Savoy Brown

Savoy Brown recorded the full-tilt, blues-rock and effectively upbeat "Train To Nowhere."

Single Releases

London
40034 "Shake Em On Down Pt. 1 & 2"   1968
40037 "Grits Ain't Groceries"/"She's Got A Ring In
       His Nose And A Ring On Her Hand"
40039 "Train To Nowhere"/"Make Up Her Mind"
40042 "I'm Tired"/"Stay With Me Baby"   1969
40057 "Poor Girl"/"Master Hare"

REISSUES

•

Many best-selling records have been continuously available as reissues on special hit label series. Recently an increased number of 50's classics were re-pressed on 45 RPM, and because of the newly awakened interest in oldies, a comparable amount of 60's material is also available. This section is a discography of currently issued 45 RPM hits by major 60's recording artists. Please consult the main text for original label details.

Early 60's Rhythm and Blues Artists

Ray Charles

ABC Oldies Treasure Chest
   1239 "Hit The Road Jack"/"Georgia On My Mind"
   1240 "Unchain My Heart'/"You Don't Know Me"
   1241 "I Can't Stop Loving You"/"You Are My Sunshine"
   1242 "Together Again"/"That Lucky Old Sun"
   1243 "Let's Go Get Stoned"/"Busted"
   1254 "Born To Lose"/"Sticks And Stones"
   1255 "Crying Time"/"One Mint Julep"
   1256 "Hard Hearted Hannah"/"Your Cheating Heart"

Sam Cooke

RCA Gold Standard
- 0566 "Twistin' The Night Away"/"You Send Me"
- 0567 "Sentimental Reasons"/"Only 16"
- 0576 "Chain Gang"/"Cupid"
- 0578 "Everybody Likes To Cha Cha Cha"/ Wonderful World"
- 0579 "Sugar Dumplin' '/"It's Got The Whole World Shakin' "
- 0705 "Bring It On Home To Me"/"Having A Party"
- 0706 "Send Me Some Lovin' "/"Another Saturday Night"
- 0707 "Good News"/"Little Red Rooster"
- 0724 "Good Times"/"Frankie And Johnny"
- 0743 "Cousin Of Mine"/"Shake"
- 0820 "A Change Is Gonna Come"/"Sad Mood"

Early 60's Rhythm and Blues Groups

The Drifters

Atlantic Oldies Series
- 13012 "Up On The Roof"/"Please Stay"
- 13013 "On Broadway"/"I've Got Sand In My Shoes"
- 13014 "Under The Boardwalk"/"Ruby Baby"
- 13015 "Saturday Night At The Movies"/"I Count The Tears"
- 13016 "Save The Last Dance For Me"/"When My Little Girl Is Smiling"
- 13017 "Some Kind Of Wonderful"/"This Magic Moment"
- 13018 "Sweets For My Sweet"/"I'll Take You Home"

Little Anthony and the Imperials

UA Silver Spotlight Series
- 117 "Goin' Out Of My Head"/"I'm On The Outside"

118   "Hurt So Bad"/"Take Me Back"

The Four Seasons

Philips Double Hit Series
44010   "Rag Doll"/"Ronnie"
44011   "Dawn"/"Save It For Me"
44017   "Sherry"/"Big Man In Town"
44018   "Big Girls Don't Cry"/"Opus 17"
44019   "Girl Come Running"/"Walk Like A Man"
44020   "Let's Hang On"/"Working My Way Back To You"
44021   "I've Got You Under My Skin"/"Bye Bye Baby"
44022   "Candy Girl"/"Peanuts"
44024   "Stay"/"Malena"

The Isley Brothers

Scepter/Wand Forever
21022   "Twist And Shout"/"Wa Watusi"

Motown Yesteryear Series
415   "This Old Heart Of Mine"/"Take Some Time Out For Love"

Radio Active Gold
31   "It's Your Thing"/"Don't Give It Away"
32   "I Turned You On"/"I Know Who You've Been Socking It To"

The Shirelles

Scepter/Wand Forever
21001   "Tonight's The Night"/"No Doubt About It"
21004   "Everybody Loves A Lover"/"Sha La La"
21006   "Dedicated To The One I Love"/"Look Away"
21007   "(Will You Love Me) Tomorrow"/"Lost Love"
21070   "Soldier Boy"/"Baby It's You"

21071 "Mama Said"/"Foolish Little Girl"

The Orlons

Abko
    4014 "South Street"/"Not Me"

The Young Rascals

Atlantic Oldies Series
    13038 "Groovin' "/"I Ain't Gonna Eat Out My Heart Anymore"
    13039 "A Beautiful Morning"/"I've Been Lonely Too Long"
    13040 "People Got To Be Free"/"How Can I Be Sure"
    13041 "A Girl Like You"/"Good Lovin' "

Motown

Barrett Strong

Motown Yesteryear Series
    504 "Money"/"Oh I Apologize"

Mary Wells

Motown Yesteryear Series
    425 "You Beat Me To The Punch"/"Two Lovers"
    426 "What's Easy For Two Is So Hard For One"/"My Guy"
    484 "Bye Bye Baby"/"The One Who Really Loves You"
    487 "Laughing Boy"/"Your Old Standby"
    489 "Once Upon A Time"/"What's The Matter With You Baby" (with Marvin Gaye)

Marvin Gaye

Motown Yesteryear Series
    405 "Stubborn Kind Of Fellow"/"Hitch Hike"

Stevie Wonder

Motown Yesteryear Series

521 "I'm Wondering"/"Hey Love"

527 "You Met Your Match"/"For Once In My Life"

Junior Walker and The All Stars

Motown Yesteryear Series

466 "Shotgun"/"Do The Boomerang"

467 "(I'm A) Road Runner"/"Shake And Fingerpop"

468 "How Sweet It Is"/"Cleo's Mood"

470 "Shoot Your Shot"/"Pucker Up Buttercup"

474 "Come See About Me"/"Hip City Pt. 2"

476 "What Does It Take (To Win Your Love)"/ "These Eyes"

479 "Gotta Hold On To This Feeling"/"Do You See My Love For You Growing"

545 "Cleo's Back"/"Hot Cha"

The Four Tops

Motown Yesteryear Series

428 "Baby I Need Your Loving"/"Without The One You Love"

429 "I Can't Help Myself"/"Ask The Lonely"

432 "Shake Me Wake Me"/"Something About You"

434 "Reach Out I'll Be There"/"Standing In The Shadows Of Love"

436 "Bernadette"/"7-Rooms Of Gloom"

438 "You Keep Running Away"/"Walk Away Renee"

440 "If I Were A Carpenter"/"I'm In A Different World"

492 "It's The Same Old Song"/"Loving You Is Sweeter Than Ever"

495 "Yesterday's Dreams"/"In These Changing Times"

Smokey Robinson and The Miracles

Motown Yesteryear Series
400 "Shop Around"/"Way Over There"
402 "What's So Good About Goodbye"/
       "Everybody's Got To Pay Some Dues"
411 "The Tracks Of My Tears"/"Ooh Baby Baby"
414 "My Girl Has Gone"/"Going To A Go Go"
417 "Come Round Here—I'm The One You
       Need"/"More Love"
505 "You've Really Got A Hold On Me"/"I'll Try
       Something New"
508 "Mickey's Monkey"/"A Love She Can Count
       On"
509 "I Like It Like That"/"I Gotta Dance To
       Keep From Crying"
514 "The Love I Saw In You Was Just A
       Mirage"/"That's What Love Is Made Of"
522 "I Second That Emotion"/"If You Can Want"
526 "Yester Love"/"Special Occasion"
528 "Baby Baby Don't Cry"/"Doggone Right"

Gladys Knight and the Pips

Motown Yesteryear Series
472 "Everybody Needs Love"/"Take Me In Your
       Arms"
473 "I Heard It Through The Grapevine"/"The
       End Of Our Road"
475 "The Nitty Gritty"/"Didn't You Know You'd
       Have To Cry"
478 "Friendship Train"/"You Need Love Like I
       Do"

The Spinners

Motown Yesteryear Series
483 "It's A Shame"/"We'll Have It Made"
491 "I'll Always Love You"/"Truly Yours"

The Marvelettes

Motown Yesteryear Series
- 401 "Please Mr. Postman"/"Twistin' Postman"
- 403 "Playboy"/"Beechwood 4-5789"
- 409 "Too Many Fish In The Sea"/"You're My Remedy"
- 412 "Danger Heartbreak Dead Ahead"/"I'll Keep Holding On"
- 506 "Strange I Know"/"As Long As I Know He's Mine"
- 507 "Locking Up My Heart"/"Forever"
- 511 "Don't Mess With Bill"/"He's A Good Guy"
- 520 "The Hunter Gets Captured By The Game"/"My Baby Must Be A Magician"
- 525 "Destination Anywhere"/"Here I Am Baby"

The Contours

Motown Yesteryear Series
- 448 "Do You Love Me"/"Shake Sherry"
- 538 "First I Look At The Purse"/"Can You Do It"

The Supremes

Motown Yesteryear Series
- 427 "Where Did Our Love Go"/"Baby Love"
- 430 "Stop In The Name Of Love"/"Back In My Arms Again"
- 431 "Nothing But Heartaches"/"I Hear A Symphony"
- 433 "My World Is Empty Without You"/"You Can't Hurry Love"
- 435 "You Keep Me Hanging On"/"Love Is Here And Now You're Gone"
- 437 "The Happening"/"Reflections"
- 439 "In And Out Of Love"/"Forever Came Today"
- 441 "I'm Gonna Make You Love Me"/"I'll Try Something New" (with The Temptations)

The Temptations

Motown Yesteryear Series

Martha and The Vandellas

Motown Yesteryear Series
- 449 "Come On And Get These Memories"/"Heat Wave"
- 451 "In My Lonely Room"/"Dancing In The Street"
- 452 "Nowhere To Run"/"My Baby Loves Me"
- 455 "I'm Ready For Love"/"Jimmy Mack"
- 459 "Love Bug Leave My Heart Alone"/"Honey Chile"
- 535 "Quicksand"/"Love (Makes Me Do Foolish Things)"

Chi-town

The Impressions

ABC Oldies Treasure Chest
- 1225 "Can't Satisfy"/"Never Let You Go"
- 1232 "Gypsy Woman"/"It's All Right"
- 1233 "Keep On Pushing"/"We're A Winner"
- 1234 "Amen"/"People Get Ready"
- 1236 "I'm So Proud"/"I Can't Stay Away From You"

ABC Goldies 45
- 1476 "Woman's Got Soul"/"You've Been Cheatin'"

Radio Active Gold
- 22 "Fool For You"/"I'm Loving Nothing"
- 23 "This Is My Country"/"My Woman's Love"
- 24 "Seven Years"/"The Girl I Find"
- 25 "Choice Of Colors"/"Mighty Mighty (Spade And Whitey)"

Jerry Butler

Mercury Celebrity Series
- 30150 "Make It Easy On Yourself"/"He Will Break Your Heart"

30151 "For Your Precious Love"/"Moon River"
30155 "Only The Strong Survive"/"Lost"
30156 "Hey Western Union Man"/"Never Give You Up"

Joe Simon

Monument Golden Series
  8915 "Nine Pound Steel"/"Hangin' On"
  8916 "The Chokin' Kind"/"Put Your Trust In Me"

Southern Rhythm and Blues

James Brown

Polydor Soul Classic
  501 "It's A Man's Man's Man's World"/"Mother Popcorn"
  502 "Cold Sweat"/"Night Train"
  503 "The Popcorn"/"Sex Machine"
  504 "Think"/"Licking Stick, Licking Stick"
  505 "Papa's Got A Brand New Bag"/"I Got The Feelin'"
  506 "I Got You"/"I Can't Stand Myself"
  507 "Money Won't Change You"/"Try Me"
  508 "Ain't It Funky Now"/"Call Me Super Bad"
  509 "Give It Up And Turn It Loose"/"Soul Power"

Joe Tex

Atlantic Oldies Series
  13110 "Hold What You've Got"/"Show Me"
  13111 "I Want To"/"Skinny Legs And All"

Ike and Tina Turner

UA Silver Spotlight Series
  119 "A Fool In Love"/"I Idolize You"
  120 "It's Gonna Work Out Fine"/"Poor Fool"
  121 "I Want To Take You Higher"/"Come Together"

122   "Tra La La La La"/"Proud Mary"

Memphis Sound

Aretha Franklin

Columbia Hall of Fame
33125   "Runnin' Out Of Fools"/"Cry Like A Baby"

Atlantic Oldies Series
13058   "Since You've Been Gone"/"Ain't No Way"
13059   "I Say A Little Prayer"/"The House That
        Jack Built"
13060   "I Never Loved A Man"/"Think"
13061   "Respect"/"You're All I Need"
13062   "Baby I Love You"/"Spanish Harlem"
13063   "A Natural Woman"/"See Saw"
13064   "Chain Of Fools"/"Bridge Over Troubled
        Water"

Wilson Pickett

Atlantic Oldies Series
13023   "I'm In Love"/"Stag-O-Lee"
13024   "In The Midnight Hour"/"634-5789"
13025   "I Found A Love"/"She's Lookin' Good"
13026   "Mustang Sally"/"Don't Knock My Love"
13028   "Funky Broadway"/"Hey Jude"
13029   "Land Of 1000 Dances"/"Engine #9"
13030   "Ninety-Nine And A Half"/"Don't Let The
        Green Grass Fool You"
13124   "Don't Fight It"/"A Man And A Half"

Otis Redding

Atlantic Oldies Series
13096   "These Arms Of Mine"/"I've Been Loving
        You Too Long"
13097   "Pain In My Heart"/"Respect"
13098   "Mr. Pitiful"/"Fa-Fa-Fa-Fa-Fa"

13099 "Satisfaction"/"Try A Little Tenderness"
13100 "(Sittin' On) The Dock Of The Bay"/"My
       Lover's Prayer"
13134 "I Can't Turn You Loose"/"Security"

Booker T & The MG's

Atlantic Oldies Series
13088 "Green Onions"/"Chinese Checkers"
13089 "Groovin' "/"Hip-Hug-Her"

Sam and Dave

Atlantic Oldies Series
13091 "Hold On I'm A Comin' "/"I Thank You"
13092 "Soul Man"/"When Something Is Wrong
       With My Baby"

Early 60's Rock and Roll Artists

Elvis Presley

RCA Gold Standard
0627 "Stuck On You"/"Fame And Fortune"
0628 "It's Now Or Never"/"A Mess Of Blues"
0629 "Are You Lonesome Tonight"/"I Gotta Know"
0630 "Surrender"/"Lonely Man"
0634 "Little Sister"/"His Latest Flame"
0635 "Can't Help Falling In Love"/"Rock-A-Hula
      Baby"
0636 "Good Luck Charm"/"Anything That's Part
      Of You"
0637 "She's Not You"/"Just Tell Her Jim Said
      Hello"
0638 "Return To Sender"/"Where Do You Come
      From"
0639 "Kiss Me Quick"/"Suspicion"
0641 "(You're The) Devil In Disguise"/"Please
      Don't Drag That String Again"
0642 "Bossa Nova Baby"/"Witchcraft"

0643 "Crying In The Chapel"/"I Believe In The Man In The Sky"
0644 "Kissin' Cousins"/"It Hurts Me"
0646 "Viva Las Vegas"/"What'd I Say"
0647 "Blue Christmas"/"Wooden Heart"
0650 "Puppet On A String"/"Wooden Heart"
0656 "Frankie And Johnny"/"Please Don't Stop Loving Me"
0657 "Love Letters"/"Come What May"
0658 "Spinout"/"All That I Am"
0662 "Big Boss Man"/"You Don't Know Me"
0663 "Guitar Man"/"High Heel Sneakers"
0664 "U.S. Male"/"Stay Away Joe"
0665 "You'll Never Walk Alone"/"We Call On Him"
0666 "Let Yourself Go"/"Your Time Hasn't Come Yet Baby"
0667 "A Little Less Conversation"/"Almost In Love"
0668 "If I Can Dream"/"Edge Of Reality"
0669 "Memories"/"Charro"
0670 "How Great Thou Art"/"His Hand In Mine"
0671 "In The Ghetto"/"Any Day Now"
0672 "Clean Up Your Own Backyard"/"The Fair Is Moving On"
0673 "Suspicious Minds"/"You'll Think Of Me"
0674 "Don't Cry Daddy"/"Rubberneckin' "
0675 "Kentucky Rain"/"My Little Friend"

Roy Orbison

Monument Golden Series
8900 "Running Scared"/"Love Hurts"
8901 "Candy Man"/"Crying"
8902 "Leah"/"Working For The Man"
8903 "Mean Woman Blues"/"Blue Bayou"
8904 "Pretty Paper"/"Beautiful Dreamer"
8906 "Only The Lonely"/"Up Town"
8907 "Dream Baby"/"I'm Hurtin"

   8908   "In Dreams"/"The Crowd"
   8910   "Oh Pretty Woman"/"It's Over"

Folk Rock

Bob Dylan

Columbia Hall of Fame
  33100   "Like A Rolling Stone"/"Rainy Day Woman
           #12 & 35"
  33108   "Just Like A Woman"/"I Want You"
  33178   "Lay Lady Lay"/"I Threw It All Away"
  33221   "Positively 4th Street"/"Subterranean
           Homesick Blues"

Neil Diamond

Solid Gold
    107   "Red Red Wine"/"Shilo"
    109   "Do It"/"I Get The Feelin' Oh No No"

Simon and Garfunkle

Columbia Hall of Fame
  33096   "Sounds Of Silence"/"Homeward Bound"
  33115   "The Dangling Conversation"/"A Hazy
           Shade Of Winter"
  33121   "At The Zoo"/"Fakin' It"
  33135   "Scarborough Fair"/"I Am A Rock"
  33143   "Mrs. Robinson"/"Old Friends/Bookends"
  33169   "The Boxer"/"Baby Driver"
  33187   "Bridge Over Troubled Water"/"Cecilia"

The Byrds

Columbia Hall of Fame
  33095   "Mr. Tambourine Man"/"All I Really Want To
           Do"
  33097   "Turn Turn Turn"/"Eight Miles High"
  33123   "So You Want To Be A Rock N Roll Star"/
           "My Back Pages"

Early California Rock and Roll

The Beach Boys

Capitol Star Line Series
- 6059 "Be True To Your School"/"In My Room"
- 6081 "Help Me Rhonda"/"Do You Wanna Dance"
- 6095 "Surfin' Safari"/"409"
- 6105 "Dance Dance Dance"/"The Warmth Of The Sun"
- 6106 "Fun Fun Fun"/"Do It Again"
- 6107 "Surfer Girl"/"Little Deuce Coupe"

The Righteous Brothers

Verve Sounds of Fame
- 140 "Ebb Tide"/"He"
- 141 "White Cliffs Of Dover"/"Just Once In My Life"

The Chambers Brothers

Columbia Hall of Fame
- 33146 "Time Has Come Today"/"I Can't Turn You Loose"

Sly and the Family Stone

Epic Memory Lane
- 2282 "Dance To The Music"/"Life"
- 2302 "Hot Fun In The Summertime"/"M'Lady"
- 2303 "Thank You For Letting Me Be Myself Again"/"Everybody Is A Star"
- 2304 "I Want To Take You Higher"/"Stand"
- 2305 "Everyday People"/"Sing A Simple Song"

Early British Rock and Roll

The Beatles

The Capitol label 45 RPM single series (except for the Capitol 6000 series which is out of print) has been entirely reissued on the Apple label complete with the original Capitol issue numbers.

The Rolling Stones

All London label singles, except for London 9641, 907 and 1022, remain available.

The Animals

MGM Golden Circle
- 179 "House Of The Rising Sun"/"I'm Crying"
- 180 "Boom Boom"/"Don't Let Me Be Misunderstood"
- 181 "Don't Bring Me Down"/"We Gotta Get Out Of This Place"
- 182 "It's My Life"/"Inside Looking Out"
- 192 "San Franciscan Nights"/"Monterey"
- 194 "Sky Pilot"/"White Horses"

The Kinks

Reprise Back To Back Hits
- 0708 "Sunny Afternoon"/"Dead End Street"
- 0712 "Who'll Be The Next In Line"/"Dedicated Followers Of Fashion"
- 0715 "A Well Respected Man"/"Set Me Free"
- 0719 "Tired Of Waiting For You"/"All Day And All Of The Night"
- 0722 "You Really Got Me"/"It's All Right"

Manfred Mann

UA Silver Spotlight Series
- 48 "Do Wah Diddy Diddy"/"Sha La La"
- 49 "Come Tomorrow"/"Pretty Flamingo"

The Yardbirds

Epic Memory Lane
- 2247 "I'm A Man"/"Shapes Of Things"

Joe Cocker

A&M Forget Me Nots
- 8541 "Delta Lady"/"Friends"
- 8546 "Cry Me A River"/"The Letter"
- 8551 "Feeling Alright"/"Black Eyed Blues"
- 8557 "She Came In The Bathroom Window"/
  "Woman To Woman"

Van Morrison

Solid Gold
- 104 "Brown Eyed Girl"/"Ro Ro Rosey"

Warner Brothers Back To Back Hits
- 7137 "Crazy Love"/"Moondance"
- 7138 "Domino"/"Into The Mystic"
- 7139 "Blue Money"/"Call Me Up In Dreamland"

San Francisco Rock

The Jefferson Airplane

RCA Gold Standard
- 0796 "Somebody To Love"/"White Rabbit"

Big Brother and The Holding Company

Columbia Hall of Fame
- 33183 "Piece Of My Heart"/"Kozmic Blues"

Los Angeles Rock

The Buffalo Springfield

Atco Oldies Series
- 13073 "For What It's Worth"/"Rock N Roll Woman"
- 13074 "Bluebird"/"Mr. Soul"

The Doors

Elektra Spun Gold
    45051 "Light My Fire"/"Love Me Two Times"
    45052 "Hello, I Love You, Won't You Tell Me
                Your Name"/"Touch Me"

Steppenwolf

ABC Goldies 45
    1433 "Born To Be Wild"/"Magic Carpet Ride"
    1444 "Rock Me"/"Monster"

Canned Heat

UA Silver Spotlight Series
        58 "On The Road Again"/"Time Was"
        59 "Going Up The Country"/"Let's Work
                Together"

British Hard Rock

The Jimi Hendrix Experience

Reprise Back To Back Hits
    0742 "All Along The Watchtower"/"Crosstown
                Traffic"

R00012 71492

473752